ADVANCE PRAISE

"*Assemblage* blends academic research with practical insights that marketers can immediately put to good use. It's a clear, concise, and actionable book."

—NIR EYAL, **Author of *Hooked* and *Indistractable***

"Want to create a transformative brand? *Assemblage* shows you how, illustrating how brands can do good for both consumers and society."

—JONAH BERGER, **Wharton Professor and Bestselling Author of *Contagious* and *The Catalyst***

"As Jeremy Bullmore famously said, 'People build brands the way birds build nests—from the scraps and straws they find lying around.' Using the model of assemblage, the art of blending fine cognacs, Emmanuel Probst provides us with a much more helpful and versatile mental model for the way brands are built in practice. It is also an approach which rings true with what we are increasingly learning about human perception and behavior."

—RORY SUTHERLAND, **Vice Chairman at Ogilvy UK**

"The only way to find brand success and growth is to reframe perceptions and decisions. Probst provides routes to doing just that. A real contribution."

—DAVID AAKER, **Vice Chairman at Prophet, Brand Strategist, and Author of *Building Strong Brands***

"*Assemblage* offers a holistic understanding of brands and perceptions—it is a must-read."

—MARTIN LINDSTROM, **New York Times Bestselling Author of *Buyology* and *The Ministry of Common Sense***

"*Assemblage* is the book I have been waiting for. Its standpoint on the marketing industry is disruptive. Its learnings are pragmatic."

—SCOTT MCDONALD, **President and CEO of the Advertising Research Foundation**

"*Assemblage* shows the transformation power of brands for both consumers and society. It's simply a must-read."

—NEIL HOYNE, **Chief Measurement Strategist at Google, Senior Fellow at Wharton, and Author of *Converted***

"Marketers and brands now have the opportunity to make a positive contribution to consumers and society. *Assemblage* is your ultimate guide for this new brand era."

—JEFF ROSENBLUM, **Founding Partner at Questus and Author of *Friction* and *Exponential***

"In an age of cynicism, where brands struggle to build trust and connection, Emmanuel Probst provides a roadmap. If you want to transform your brand so that it might transform consumers and society, you must read *Assemblage*."

—LAURA GASSNER OTTING, ***Washington Post* Bestselling Author of *Limitless***

"*Assemblage* uses psychology, art, culture, and real-life examples to examine how brands can approach marketing to make a powerful and positive impact on the world. I highly recommend it for marketing professionals and consumers alike."

—SHONALI BURKE, **Chief Marketing Officer at Arena Stage**

ASSEMBLAGE

ASSEMBLAGE

THE ART
AND SCIENCE
OF BRAND
TRANSFORMATION

—

DR. EMMANUEL PROBST

IDEAPRESS
PUBLISHING

WASHINGTON, D.C.

IDEAPRESS
PUBLISHING

Published in the United States by Ideapress Publishing.

Ideapress Publishing | www.ideapresspublishing.com

All trademarks are the property of their respective companies.

Cover Design by Faceout Studio, Amanda Hudson

Cataloging-in-Publication Data is on file with the Library of Congress.

ISBN: 978-1-64687-125-4

Proudly Printed in the USA

Special Sales
Ideapress Books are available at a special discount for bulk purchases for sales promotions and premiums, or for use in corporate training programs. Special editions, including personalized covers, a custom foreword, corporate imprints, and bonus content, are also available.

1 2 3 4 5 6 7 8 9 10

Je veux être utile
À vivre et à rêver

I want to be useful
To live and to dream

—Julien Clerc

CONTENTS

✦ ✦ ✦

Part 1 | How Brands Can Transform Me

Chapter 1: We Are Antiheroes, Villains, and Saviors   **13**

Chapter 2: We Seek Reassurance about Our Past, Present, and Future   **27**

✵   ✵   ✵

Part 2 | How Brands Can Transform My World

✦ ✦ ✦

Part 3 | How Brands Can Transform the World

INTRODUCTION

A white dot is blinking across the screen from left to right. It opens up to reveal a gun barrel's interior. From the point of view of a presumed assassin, the camera follows as James Bond walks. Bond suddenly becomes aware of the threat and stops at the center of the screen. He turns to the camera and shoots his gun directly toward it, causing a blood-red wash (the gunman bleeding) to run down the screen.

Since the release of *Dr. No* in 1962, the James Bond movie franchise has generated over $8 billion in box office revenue across 27 movies.[1] To put things in perspective, it is estimated that half of the world's population has seen at least one James Bond film.[2] Over the years, this cinematic embodiment of British sophistication secured numerous product placements and brand partnerships with the likes of Omega, Aston Martin, and Tom Ford, along with more mainstream brands such as Michael Kors, Heineken, and La Perla.

But over the last 60 years, the James Bond brand and its associated partnerships could easily have fallen by the wayside. Instead, it evolved by constantly assembling original brand assets with newer attributes that aligned with Bond's contemporary societal and cultural environment. As such, James Bond's constant distinctive brand assets include the opening scene, his Aston Martin, tuxedo, and vodka martini. Other aspects and characters of the franchise have evolved as well: Miss Moneypenny (M's secretary) is now embodied by a Black actress (Naomie Harris). James Bond's enemies evolved from the Eastern bloc to North Korea to an over-arching virtual evil. Q (who creates and delivers James Bond's gadgets) is now openly gay, which does not phase James Bond or Moneypenny.

The James Bond brand is an assemblage. It combines old and new attributes to engage fans and brand partners over time by staying relevant and attuned to its sociocultural and economic environment. Today, assemblages have become critical to the success of any brand. Indeed, people expect brands to not only provide them with products and services but also make a positive impact on society and the economy. Just like the James Bond franchise, brands that evolve through assemblages will thrive, while brands that don't will become irrelevant and eventually die.

This book will show you how to emulate the Bond assemblage. It will teach you the art and science of assembling brands that thrive by transforming their customers and making a positive impact on the world.

In the 1960s, advertising legend David Ogilvy asserted that senior advertising executives and so-called creative people did not have a monopoly on great ideas. He argued that some of the best ideas come from junior employees, researchers, and everyday people. I wrote *Assemblage* with Ogilvy in mind.

Through this exploratory journey, you will learn from talented marketers such as the team behind James Bond, the Houdini brothers, Dr. Evil, Lil Miquela, Taylor Swift, and DJ Khaled. You'll also discover case studies from a range of big and small brands, including Gucci, Ruinart, Omsom, and Farrow & Ball.

Whether you are a marketer or not, *Assemblage* will give you the confidence to create great brands that drive profit for your business, feel personal and relevant to your customers, and make a positive impact on society.

What is assemblage?

Assemblage is a French word that refers to the art and science of blending different eaux-de-vies (brandies) before bottling cognac. It is the craft of the maître de chai (also known as the master blender or cellar master) to select brandies from dozens of samples and craft a unique cognac. Much like the "nose" of a perfume house, the master blender determines the best possible combination of blends of various ages and crus that will constitute the character of the cognac.

Assemblage is a subtle combination of terroir (land), barrels, and equipment like the still. The art of assemblage combines what nature brings—the harvests—along with empirical knowledge of the craft. The master blender also relies on oenologists, scientists who leverage their skills in biology and chemistry to establish processes and bring distinctive styles to the finished product. In the final assemblage, there will be traces of the ancestral cognac, some of them 100 years old.

Assemblage is also a metaphor for building successful brands.

- Like a brand manager, the master blender is responsible for the consistency of the product over time. They do not just select but also oversee the vineyard, the harvest, and the brandy's aging process.

- The master blender combines rigor, precision, and intuition to create a unique product that will stand out. They are visionaries who anticipate the product's development through the assemblage.

- The master blender must also listen to consumers to understand how their tastes evolve and what products they are most likely to buy.

- In winemaking, as in marketing, money only goes so far: The quality of the raw product is just as important as a network of trusted suppliers and the audacious vision of the master blender.

In *brand assemblages*, elements are brought together, shaped, and ordered by actors that have the authority and legitimacy to do so. Assemblages can include people, physical features, and even technologies that allow the consumer to access the brand and its products.

- Brands are dynamic assemblages of social and cultural attributes that form clusters of association and meaning.

- Brand components can be added or removed. As such, the art and science of assemblage assess the fit between different brand elements to ensure brand longevity by adding elements to an existing framework the consumer is already familiar with.

- Stories that connect brands to a wider sociocultural context are central to establishing consumer engagement.

- Brands are dynamic and fluid; new components to assemblages can help stabilize or destabilize the brand. Understanding and balancing assemblages allow companies to balance continuity and change.

Assemblages go through two articulations. First, the attributes, drawn from a wide set of materials, are quantified. In the second articulation, these materials are coded—that is, the assemblage is solidified and endorses a specific meaning.[3]

Just like in wine assemblages, components of brand assemblages have "capacities" to evolve and transform when they interact with other elements. For example, water has the capacity to boil at 212°F, but this capacity only manifests when the water is heated.

When the audience is involved in the assemblage, people find comfort and satisfaction in contributing to the brand, imagining other possible variations, and predicting attributes that will be part of the assemblage's next iteration.

Just like master blenders collect and combine eaux-de-vies, I spent the last 20 years researching and experimenting with how we can build brands that are more meaningful for consumers and make a positive impact on society, the economy, and the environment. I collected hundreds of data points, insights, and ideas through my doctoral research in consumer psychology and interactions with executives at Fortune 500 brands, students from my Consumer Market Research class at UCLA, and mentors. As such, this book is my own assemblage of the elements that are most important in creating strong brands.

What makes assemblage so difficult?

Today, brands no longer have a single meaning. Brand identity is defined in specific contexts, and actors (consumers, citizens, the public, key opinion formers, businesses) give meaning to brands in context. Brands are continuously open to contestations from consumers that shape their narratives, meanings, and relationships with these brands. In particular, we shape, contest, and augment the identity of brands on social media through our own manifestation of the brand. As such, we create a narrative by navigating the brand's primary narrative and modifying it through our creative posts and interaction with others.

Consumer-driven cultural moments can also upend brands. This leads to costly and risky marketing efforts to create new brands or significantly reposition existing ones. Think of the Cleveland Indians, Victoria's Secret, Uncle Ben's, or Aunt Jemima. These brands had to overhaul their identities in response to mounting criticism from the public who deemed them offensive and disrespectful of Native Americans, women, and people of color.

Rather than controlling the brand narrative, brand managers now monitor, moderate, and channel brand contestation from consumers. Brand managers increasingly endorse the role of brand ambassadors who must listen to and represent the brand's audience. Many marketers are loath to admit that brands are now "open source" and struggle to manage the tension between giving away and retaining control.

Consumers now have access to an abundance of options at their fingertips, which makes it harder to choose brands. These options also make it difficult for marketers and their brands to stand out. In *The Paradox of Choice*, American psychologist Barry Schwartz reveals that having too many options creates problems rather than solutions.[4] Scrolling through thousands of swim trunks on Amazon may feel empowering but actually triggers anxiety. By way of illustration, an average Barnes & Noble store carries about 100,000 titles; Amazon carries an inventory of approximately five million titles.[5] The same reasoning applies to music; your typical Walmart store carries about 55,000 tracks while Spotify stores about 70 million tracks.[6]

From *going* shopping to always shopping

We no longer need to carve out time to go to physical stores or visit online merchant platforms; mobile technology and social media have integrated shopping into our daily lives. Social apps feed us with personalized inspirations and curated recommendations, making social commerce the new storefront. Content creators and influencers play an important role in this process, presenting us with brands and products we were not looking for in a personal and organic fashion.[7]

The infinite scroll

As we scroll down a page on many websites, content continuously loads at the bottom without the need to click on the next page. That's the *infinite scroll*—a web design practice that has become standard across social media platforms, blogs, and e-commerce websites. The infinite scroll is designed to pull us in and keep us scrolling; there is no natural stopping point. Aza Raskin designed the infinite scroll in 2006 with the earnest intention to eliminate friction for users; because we are already scrolling, chances are we want to access more of the same content.

Raskin notes that tech firms encourage us to scroll more to drive usage and financial gains.

> It's as if they're taking behavioral cocaine and just sprinkling it all over your interface, and that's the thing that keeps you coming back and back and back. Behind every

screen on your phone, there are literally a thousand engineers that have worked on this thing to try to make it maximally addicting.[8]

Raskin said he did not set up his design to get people addicted and feels guilty about the unforeseen impact of his invention.

Just as with the paradox of choice outlined above, the infinite scroll eventually results in a frustrating experience for users. We naturally expect a sense of progress and to reach an end. The infinite scroll disorients us.

More is less

Overwhelmed with all these offerings, many people no longer trust brands or marketers. In 2021, Havas Media Group surveyed over 395,000 people worldwide to gauge their sentiment toward two thousand brands.[9] The report showed that we've entered the "age of cynicism"; trust in brands is at its lowest point since Havas started tracking brand trust in 2009. Specifically, the study shows that 75 percent of brands could disappear overnight and people would easily replace them. Further, 71 percent of participants have little faith that brands deliver on their promises, and only 34 percent believe brands are transparent about their commitments and promises. Last but not least, less than half of brands (47 percent) are seen as trustworthy.

The three dimensions of the assemblage method

To succeed in the long run, brands must assemble components that support the individual ("me"), that individual's close group ("my world"), and the society and culture they live in ("the world").

By taking you through these three dimensions, *Assemblage* will show you the path to building brands that lead to positive transformation for consumers and society. The assemblage method consists of nine key aspects, organized in three parts, that fulfill "me, my world, and the world."

PART 1 | HOW BRANDS CAN TRANSFORM ME

In the first chapter, we uncover why we relate to antiheroes, villains, and saviors and how successful brands harness these archetypes to make the consumer (not the brand) triumphant. Chapter 2 explains why and how we seek reassurance about our past, present, and future. Chapter 3 deciphers the complexity of managing our real self (who we are in real life), digital self (how we present ourselves on social media), and virtual self (our avatar in the metaverse). Chapter 4 shows us how brands should establish and prioritize personal relationships with their audience to make their businesses human in the eyes of consumers.

PART 2 | HOW BRANDS CAN TRANSFORM MY WORLD

The fifth chapter, "Perception Is the Truth," uncovers how we construct truth based on our perception of the world, the information we are exposed to, and what we want the truth to be. In Chapter 6, we look at how the remix economy enables all of us to be discovered and to monetize our skills.

PART 3 | HOW BRANDS CAN TRANSFORM THE WORLD

Chapter 7 further asserts the power of the people as brands become less of a dominating force. Indeed, everybody has the power to advocate for brands, talk back at them, or even cancel them. Chapter 8 shows how brands must be "glocal"—supporting local culture and merchants while scaling their presence globally. Chapter 9 shows a better, more sustainable, path to consumption and brand building.

After covering these three dimensions, the final chapter enables us to learn from assemblers that have mastered the art and science of assemblage, even though most of them are not marketers per se.

You can read *Assemblage* cover to cover (and I hope you will!) or skim chapters, case studies, anecdotes, and the key learning outcomes outlined at the end of each chapter.

A humble word of caution

As you have already realized, this book looks at marketing through many unconventional and arguably provocative examples. Among these examples are religious leaders, controversial politicians, hip-hop artists, and villains. These examples are presented through the lenses of marketing, brand strategy, and consumerism. As such, I do not endorse (nor necessarily condemn) these personalities and their practices. *Assemblage* is written with respect for everyone's culture, origins, beliefs, political opinions, and sexual orientations.

PART 1

HOW BRANDS CAN TRANSFORM ME

WE ARE ANTIHEROES, VILLAINS, AND SAVIORS

Heroes, villains, saviors, and antiheroes are all relatable and sympathetic in their own ways.

In marketing, the consumer should be positioned as the hero, not the brand.

We all have instinctive and primitive desires such as safety, freedom, control, and belonging. These basic human emotions can be aligned with matching "archetypes," which are the personification of these behaviors. An archetype contains images, emotions, and scripts for action. The heroes, antiheroes, villains, and saviors presented in this chapter provide us with a road map to accurately appeal to our primitive desires.

The hero

The hero is someone who dreams, acts on those dreams, rationalizes his action, and shares the means to his fulfillment. He is heroic for helping others uncover themselves.[1] The audience must always know who the hero is, what he wants, who the hero has to defeat, what tragic things will happen if he fails, and what wonderful things will happen if he triumphs.[2]

Consumption is heroic, with consumers as actors playing different roles with the aid of scripts, props, and costumes, all provided through advertising and material goods. First, the hero separates himself from reality. That's his "call to adventure." Then, he enters uncharted territory. Finally, he conquers and returns.

In marketing, the consumer must be positioned as the hero, with the brand only there to help and support him. Over time, consumers who feel empowered to become heroes will develop a stronger connection with the brand.

The antihero

An antihero is a main character in a movie, story, or drama who lacks the qualities we conventionally attribute to a hero, such as integrity, courage, strength, and idealism. Antiheroes are part villain, part hero, who often break the law, seek revenge, and engage in antisocial behavior to achieve their goals. Examples of antiheroes in television and film include Tony Soprano (*The Sopranos*), Don Draper *(Mad Men)*, and Walter White (*Breaking Bad*).

We like antiheroes because they are flawed and morally complex, making them closer to us than heroes and villains. We live vicariously through antiheroes because they reject the constraints and expectations society imposes on us. We accept that they mess up now and again but side with them as long as they are making progress. Often, antiheroes have experienced some personal misfortune or prejudice that explains their behavior and fuels their progress. In the TV show *Mad Men*, Don Draper, who constantly cheats and drinks, grew up in a brothel during the Great Depression. James Bond is not just an assassin; he is also an orphan and a widower. The painful injustices endured by antiheroes help spark passion for their cause.

How Equinox appeals to the antihero in us

The fitness industry is ridden with clichés: the buff guy who seems to spend his life on the gym floor and looks down on other members, the thirty-something female lifting light weights wearing yoga pants, and of course, a group of sweaty people punching the air in an aerobics class. Rather than addressing these perceptions head-on, most health clubs default to bland taglines.

Enter the high-end lifestyle and fitness brand Equinox, which stands out with unconventional, sometimes bizarre advertising campaigns. In 2016, the brand challenged what it called "a modern-day aversion to loyalty." In 2015, Equinox rolled out its "Equinox made me do it" campaigns, featuring uninhibited antiheroes living a provoked life: a woman escorted out of a mansion by two security guards, presumably after trying to break in; a man in a suit and tie jumping a wired fence; a model in business attire with a razor in hand and a freshly shaved head; a man cross-dressed in a woman's office clothes.

Besides its artistic value and provocative stance, Equinox campaigns prompted its core audience of elite, overachieving professionals to reveal their mischievous, daring, antihero selves. As such, Equinox is transformative, empowering members to fulfill their quest of becoming who they want to be.

> I like flaws and feel more comfortable around people
> who have them. I myself am made entirely of flaws,
> stitched together with good intentions.
>
> —AUGUSTEN BURROUGHS, AMERICAN WRITER

We are shifting toward more inclusive heroes

US Census data shows that in the past decade, people who identify as Hispanic, Asian, or multiracial are driving much of the population growth, while the white population has declined for the first time in history.[3] Brands must authentically reflect these diverse backgrounds and experiences to connect with their future customers.

Studies show that younger generations take greater notice of inclusive advertising when they consider a purchase. In the auto sector, for example, 35 percent of 18- to 25-year-old consumers notice inclusive advertising versus 18 percent of those over 45. In beauty and personal care, it is 28 percent versus 10 percent.[4] Customers are also more loyal to brands that commit to addressing inequalities, whether it's using diverse suppliers, considering people with disabilities, or something else. As such, brands reduce the cultural and demographic distance between their marketers and the consumer audiences they aspire to reach.

The Dove "reverse selfie" campaign celebrates women and their "imperfections"

Dove, through its "campaign for real beauty," is on a mission to build the self-confidence of women and children. In 2021, the brand launched its "reverse selfie" campaign, which zooms in on the effect that image manipulation has on young girls.

In its "reverse selfie" ad, Dove reveals each alteration done to a photo in reverse, from the picture posted on social media to the true subject of the selfie: a young girl in her bedroom with many skin and aesthetic "imperfections." Dove's campaign was prompted by research showing that girls who regularly manipulate their photos have lower self-esteem than those who don't. This same research shows that 80 percent of Canadian girls age 13 and over have downloaded or used an app to alter their appearance.[5]

"We're committed to redefining beauty, challenging stereotypes, and celebrating what makes women unique," says Ashley Boyce, marketing manager for skin cleansing and Dove master brand at Unilever Canada. "We need to raise young people's self-esteem so they can navigate social media in a way which is positive and creative."[6]

The underdog effect

The underdog effect refers to people or brands that overcome seemingly insurmountable challenges and difficulties. Americans especially love stories of underdogs—who are expected to lose—which is pervasive in literature, film, politics, sports, religion, and, of course, marketing.

We are often drawn to underdogs specifically because they are the ones that are disadvantaged or unlikely to prevail. In *David and Goliath: Underdogs, Misfits, and the Art of Battling Giants*, Malcolm Gladwell brings forth several underdogs who end up triumphant: a girls' basketball team that succeeds by exploiting their opponents' conventional tactics; an oncologist who came from extreme poverty during the Depression era.

The notion of being an underdog is often manipulated to make something or someone more appealing. In politics, Barack Obama, Hillary Clinton, Donald Trump, and many others position themselves as underdogs based on their name, humble beginnings, or their exclusion by the establishment.

The underdog effect permeates the business world and particularly tech firms in Silicon Valley: Apple, Microsoft, HP, Google, and Amazon reportedly all started in garages. This likely explains why so many co-working spaces and so-called incubators harbor garage doors and a stripped-down, concrete, industrial feel. (The garage where Steve Jobs and Steve Wozniak reportedly started Apple was deemed a historical site in 2013.[7] Wozniak admits that Apple starting in a garage was "a bit of a myth . . . we did no designs there, no white-boarding, no prototyping, no planning of products. We did no manufacturing there."[8])

The villains and why we are attracted to them

Although we'd be repulsed by people in the real world that display immoral behavior, we are attracted to fictional villains like Voldemort and Darth Vader. These villains don't threaten our self-esteem and tend to desensitize us to immorality, revealing our "dark side."[9] Rebecca Krause, an academic who researches our relationship with heroes and villains, says they provide a "safe haven" for comparison with ourselves because they are separate from reality.

> When people feel safe, they are more interested in comparisons to negative characters that are similar to themselves in other respects.[10] For example, people who see themselves as tricky and chaotic may feel especially drawn to the character of the Joker in the *Batman* movies, while a person who shares Lord Voldemort's intellect and ambition may feel more drawn to that character in the *Harry Potter* series. . . . Perhaps fiction provides a way to engage with the dark aspects of your personality without making you question whether you are a good person in general.[11]

In James Bond movies, the villain is often the key focus of the plot. American screenwriter Michael Wilson explains that when creating a Bond villain, his team thinks, "'What is the world afraid of? Where are we headed?' Then, we try to create a villain that is the physical embodiment of that fear."[12] As such, each villain mirrors geopolitical shifts to stay relevant in contemporary culture. That's how the franchise moved from the Soviet Union to North Korea to a broader terror group.

> You see, why does it feel so good?
> So good to be bad
> —DAVID GUETTA AND SHOWTEK, DJS

Dr. EV-il, a sympathetic villain to the rescue of General Motors

Since its inception in 1908, auto giant General Motors has sold exclusively gas-powered cars. Today, GM is transforming its brands and operations to meet the booming demand for electric vehicles and accommodate existing and upcoming legislative imperatives. GM recently debuted "Everybody In," a new marketing campaign that sets an optimistic tone for the car manufacturer's EV future.

For the 2021 Super Bowl, General Motors and its agency, McCann Detroit, created an ad inspired by the *Austin Powers* franchise. The spot opens with "Dr. EV-il"—EV being a reference to electric vehicles—declaring his complete takeover of GM from the top floor of the automaker's Detroit HQ, with the intent, of course, to achieve world domination. This evil intent is turned into great news thanks to the automaker's EV production platform and battery systems that will power the entire operation. Unimpressed with his entourage's plan to "reduce carbon emissions," Dr. EV-il eventually takes ownership of GM's vision to go all-electric, ultimately accepting a new challenge: to destroy the world, he must first prevent climate change by reducing tailpipe emissions.

The saviors

Steve Jobs

The savior is an individual who can always be relied upon in a crisis. In 1997, Apple's computers were considered "toys" that were incapable of "real" computing. Steve Jobs had just made his comeback as interim CEO and retained TBWA/Chiat/Day to create the "Think different" campaign. The big idea for these ads was that, like Apple, all great thinkers (Albert Einstein, Muhammad Ali, John Lennon, etc.) had an amazing vision, yet all of them were given unflattering labels at one point or another.[13] "Here's to the crazy ones. The misfits. The rebels. The troublemakers [. . .] Because the people who are crazy enough to think they can change the world are the ones who do," says the ad.

> What does Steve do exactly? He can't even code.[14]
> —APPLE EMPLOYEE

Jeff Bezos and Elon Musk promise life on Mars

The world's wealthiest and most influential entrepreneurs have plans that go well beyond market domination. Jeff Bezos believes that our growing energy demands will outweigh its limited supply on Earth. Bezos predicts a rather apocalyptic future on planet Earth, where climate change will make the planet inhabitable. Energy in short supply, the population will no longer be able to travel, and rationing and starvation will follow.

> We have to go to space to save Earth.
> —JEFF BEZOS[15]

With these concerns about Earth in mind, Bezos founded Blue Origin, which aims to enable future generations to live and work in space to preserve the Earth. Bezos believes these colonies will grow without any earthly constraints. "We can have a trillion humans in the solar system, which means we'd have a thousand Mozarts and a thousand Einsteins. This would be an incredible civilization," claims Bezos.[16] For now, Blue Origin is working on developing reusable launch vehicles for its civil, commercial, and defense customers. Fellow billionaire Elon Musk also hopes to escape the limitations of planet Earth by colonizing Mars. His devoted followers, the "Musketeers," believe Musk will save the world and is on a mission to make the planet a better place.

Hummer: From hero to villain to savior

The Gulf War of 1991 saw widespread use of the high mobility multipurpose wheeled vehicle, better known as the Humvee. AM General, which produced the military version of the vehicle, started working on a civilian version of the Humvee in the late 1980s, which it eventually commercialized to the public under the brand name "Hummer" in 1992.

In June 1990, Arnold Schwarzenegger was shooting the movie *Kindergarten Cop* in Oregon when he saw a Humvee in a caravan of military vehicles. Schwarzenegger thought the vehicle looked "ballsy" and became obsessed with it. "He just went ape for that machine," said his agent Lou Pitt. "It was big, it was unique, and it was something that was larger than him. He just loved the vehicle and what it could do and what it looked like."[17] Schwarzenegger convinced the manufacturers to produce a version of the Humvee for the civilian market. Already famous for bodybuilding, acting, and his interest in cigars, Schwarzenegger became the poster child of the macho man and an integral part of the success of the gas-guzzling SUV.

In 1994, "metrosexual" was coined, referring to an urban, well-groomed male that was threatening traditional masculinity.[18] The Hummer became the obvious choice to express heterosexuality, running tag lines such as "reclaim your masculinity" and "restore the balance." In the early 2000s, the Hummer became a symbol of excess and militarist aesthetic, eventually turning into a cultural phenomenon.

Then came the financial crisis of 2009. The tough economic conditions, coupled with the sharp increase in gas prices, considerably impacted Hummer's sales. General Motors, which had by then filed for Chapter 11, announced in June 2009 that the Hummer would be discontinued.

From a symbol of power, the Hummer had become a cartoonish relic of masculinity and was receiving increased criticism for its contribution to pollution. The car had become uselessly macho.

Today, it is revived through a new type of heroic narrative—saving the environment. In January 2020, General Motors announced the relaunch of the once gas-guzzling SUV: the Electric Hummer (formally known as the GMC Hummer EV). This new version combines all the attributes that a car needs today to make the driver feel like a hero: It is authentic, in line with the rugged look and feel of the original edition. Also, it is as big and as rugged as the original, capable of enduring the most challenging terrain. Although, as previously described in the Dr. EV-il example, drivers of the new Hummer EV will feel empowered to help save the planet, as the new version of the once gas-guzzling military vehicle no longer burns any fuel.

Marketing tactics from cult leaders

Whether we like it or not, cults are very effective in building a following of devotees. Beyond the manipulative and unethical aspects of cults, there is a lot we can learn from cult leaders.

Provide clear and simple answers

A cult leader is the only one who can provide cookie-cutter answers to followers' existential questions; shortcuts to help their followers make quick judgments without even processing the information. Then, repetition (or what we in marketing elegantly call *frequency of exposure*) leads devotees to recall and accept these answers as universal truths.

Urgency and scarcity

Cult leaders rely on scarcity and urgency to prompt devotees to take action. The phenomenon is described as FOMO, or fear of missing out, in popular culture and marketing. Learning outcome: Build limited series and exclusive access to products and promotions for your most valuable clients.

Every hero needs his villain

Cult leaders promote a sense of adversity toward outside enemies. They cultivate an "us versus them" mindset that demonizes nonmembers and, in turn, strengthens the bonds of devotees.

This is the core idea behind tribal marketing—single out a brand's audience based on members' affinities, interests, and shared beliefs. Nonusers miss out on the benefits of the products. Users or members of the tribe feel superior to groups of outside nonusers.

Lock your audience in a funnel

One thing multi-level marketing, airline loyalty programs, and Scientology have in common is that they funnel people into an ascending scheme that usually starts with a freebie or something very easy to achieve. Once in the funnel, members are constantly upsold on the benefits of progressing to the next tier. Scientology puts its members through 15 levels that can take decades and hundreds of thousands of dollars to achieve. In a similar vein, many members of airline and hotel programs end up booking flights and rooms that are more expensive than competing alternatives to ensure they secure a certain status tier in the brand's loyalty program.

Emphasize the emotional over the functional

Cults appeal to pathos—using emotions to persuade their audience through metaphors, storytelling, and the passionate delivery of a speech or personal anecdote. They tap into their followers' desire for belonging, acceptance, security, and love. In contrast, ethos persuades through credibility and trust, while a logo relies on evidence and logical reasoning.

KEY TAKEAWAYS ✦ ✦ ✦

- Practically all hero stories follow the same narrative: First, the hero separates himself from reality. That's his "call to adventure." Then, he enters uncharted territory. Finally, he conquers and returns.

- Consumption is heroic; consumers play different roles with the aid of scripts, props, and costumes, all provided through advertising and material goods.

- Antiheroes are part villains, part heroes, who often break the law, seek revenge, and engage in antisocial behavior to achieve their goals.

- Just like us, antiheroes wrestle with their own demons and try to learn and develop despite their flaws. We accept that they mess up now and again; we can side with them as long as they are making progress.

- In marketing, the consumer must be positioned as the hero with the brand only to help and support him.

- The savior can always be relied upon in a crisis, is full of desire to help others, and will save them from great trouble. In certain forms of marketing, Jeff Bezos is portrayed as a modern-day savior who preaches the gospel of the apocalypse and promises to deliver us from evil.

- Consumers are actors that play the role of the hero to satisfy their ego. When identifying with a brand and consuming its product, we hope it will transform us into a better, or even heroic, person.

WE SEEK REASSURANCE ABOUT OUR PAST, PRESENT, AND FUTURE

As the world we live in feels unsafe and unstable, we seek permanence and reassurance about life and death.

Rather than seek refuge, we sometimes escape the world through daydreams, experiences, and hobbies.

We're increasingly exhausted and depressed by daily activities and the world we live in. Even before the pandemic, antidepressant use among US adults had increased from 10.6 percent in 2009 to 13.8 percent in 2018.[1] By December 2020, this rate had almost quadrupled (42.4 percent).[2] In the meantime, we are aware of the importance of our mental well-being; an Ipsos Global Advisor study (2022) reveals that for 79 percent of people, mental and physical health are equally important.

Worried about the present and future, we find comfort in objects, places, and cultural artifacts from the past that take us back to a place that is familiar and reassuring. The type of music we listen to exemplifies this reasoning. According to research firm Luminate, the streaming of current music (released within the last 18 months) declined in 2021.[3] This led to an increase in the streaming of old favorites. These "catalog" tracks comprised 70 percent of the streaming universe in 2021 versus 65 percent in

2020. Meanwhile, vinyl sales grew over 50 percent to 41.7 million units in 2021, outpacing CD sales (40.6 million units) for the first time in MRC's data history (since 1991).

Places from the past as markers of permanence

Beyond music, we also find refuge in places that have been converted to serve a new purpose.

Designed in 1912, the church of Santa Barbara in Llanera, Asturias, was left abandoned for years. A collective called the "Church Brigade" raised funds and secured a partnership with Red Bull to salvage the church and turn it into a skate park called Kaos Temple. Artist Okuda San Miguel was commissioned to decorate the walls and vaulted ceilings with his signature colorful geometric figures. In Regents Park, London, another church, St. Bede's Hall, turned into the Engine Room, a health club specializing in small groups and personal training. The architecture was preserved, but the stained glass now shows athletes performing Olympian sports. In Seattle, a 1923 colonial-style building that was once a funeral home became a bar called "the Pine Box." The bar itself and most of the tables are built from reclaimed coffin cabinets; a ceramic block by the draft screens was part of the original urn storage. In Boston, the Liberty Hotel is the transformation of the Charles Street Jail, built in 1851. The 298 rooms and suites were once cells hosting Boston's most notorious criminals. The jail's granite exterior and expansive interiors remain mostly unchanged, along with the central atrium that now constitutes the core of the hotel.

These places unconsciously help us defy death by serving as markers of permanence between the past, present, and future. The growing demand for bunker-type dwellings best exemplifies our longing for a utopian world where time stops and we are protected from diseases, disasters, and evils.

Bunkers

Preppers, also called survivalists, are a subculture of people who prepare for natural disasters, wars, nuclear attacks, and other disruptions of the social, economic, or political order. Preppers emphasize self-reliance, acquiring survival knowledge and skills, and stockpiling supplies.

The movement began in the Cold War era, when civil defense programs promoted public atomic bomb shelters along with training films, such as *Duck and Cover,* that taught children and adults what to do in the event of a nuclear explosion.

A supposedly effective way to shelter oneself from the insecurities of the outside world is to retire in an underground bunker. Since the outbreak of the pandemic, people have been acquiring new bunkers but also upgrading existing ones or putting more food in storage.[4] More people are anxious to protect their families from the turbulent world; others are just keen to live off the grid. Some shelter companies even market military-grade materials, such as NBC (nuclear, biological, and chemical) air filtration systems, six-point locking systems, and gas-tight, waterproof doors.

The Survival Condo is perhaps the most lavish and sophisticated bunker in the world. Set up in central Kansas and once a Cold War US government missile silo, now it's a 60-meter, 15-story luxury development, where up to 75 people could live self-sufficiently for five years. The Survival Condo includes a supermarket, indoor pool, pet park, and climbing wall. Most interestingly, the developers believe that the key to well-being underground is to create an illusion of normal life. The psychologist who worked with developers suggested outfitting the supermarket like a miniature Whole Foods, with tile floors and nicely presented cases.

Bunkers are not exclusive to the wealthy. Northeast Bunkers from Pittsfield, Maine, designs and builds underground bunkers priced around $25,000. That said, a bunker often includes more extensive amenities such as a security room, weapons room, storage room, panic room, and blast doors.

Friends, the depiction of timeless and effortless adult friendships

We also seek a sense of permanence and reassurance in our social relationships; this explains the enduring success of *Friends,* the famous American sitcom. Young adults Monica, Rachel, Phoebe, Ross, Chandler, and Joey have very different goals and occupations yet all relate to one another and comfort each other in tough times.

Why do we still watch *Friends* nearly 20 years after it ended? First, despite social media, it is harder and harder to make friends. Three in ten millennials always or often feel lonely; 22 percent say they have no friends at all.[5] Unlike in *Friends,* real-life friendships are tinted with conflicts, jealousies, and reconciliations. Life is also made of events that prompt us to move to a new city, separate, or move in with a new partner, while in *Friends,* the characters are anchored to a central location. *Friends* fulfills the sense of belonging, permanence, and timelessness most of us long for.

We seek pleasure and instant satisfaction

According to Freud, the pleasure principle is the driving force of our identity, which seeks instant gratification of all our needs, wants, and urges. It is the most basic and animalistic part of our personality. Some needs cannot always be satisfied the moment we feel them, or else we'd often behave inappropriately. Our ego helps ensure our needs are met but in a socially acceptable way. We escape the constraints of reality through our imagination and fantasies.

Fantasy: An escape from the dullness of our daily lives and dull products. In new worlds, we are free to go beyond the limitations of what we know and believe. Separate from the real world, fantasy worlds are places of escape and refuge, free of imperfections. They create the illusion of being removed from real life, its worries, and real consumption.

Imagination: Involves our thoughts, images, emotions, and bodily sensations. Imagination is "the mental capacity for experiencing, constructing, or manipulating "mental imagery" [. . .] for a much wider range of mental activities dealing with the non-actual, such as supposing and pretending."[6] Our imagination enables us to experience things in the absence of their material presence.

We find this pleasure and gratification in painful experiences

It has become difficult to be ourselves so we seek to step out of our skin in one way or another; a phenomenon sociologist David Le Breton called "whitening" in reference to the void suggested by the color white. This is one reason why more Americans are going through painful experiences such as getting tattooed: in 2012, 21 percent of the population had at least one tattoo. In 2022, this number has reached 30 percent and is expected to continue to grow for years to come.[7] Interestingly, the tattoo removal market[8] is also expected to grow by 6.5 percent by 2026. Traditional marketing tends to position pain as purely negative, assuming consumers are supposed to seek pleasure and avoid pain. However, consumers increasingly search for painful experiences to suspend the mind for a while.

Other painful and exhausting consumer experiences are also on the rise:

- Cryotherapy (a liquid nitrogen-powered chamber that lowers the skin temperature to 30°) is expected to grow to over $390 million by 2030, up from $213 in 2020.[9]

- Obstacle course racing, which involves overcoming obstacles such as "ladder to hell" and "electroshock therapy,"[10] is making a comeback after the pandemic. Interestingly, Tough Mudder primarily markets its races to white-collar professionals, who are more likely to suffer from their responsibilities and sedentary lives.

What tattoos, cryotherapy, and obstacle course racing all have in common is providing an emotional release and a form of freedom from the constraints of the world and our own identity. These "whitening" experiences enable us to escape from family and professional responsibilities, and we are expected to showcase our successes on social media.

Why we seek pain

Pain acts as a self-shattering episode: it breaks the "weariness of the self, which is the burden of constantly having to deal with social expectations and representing oneself."[11]

- Pain forces us to slow down physically and concentrate on ourselves, moving from an external to an internal focus. A study of the pilgrims walking the ancient Christian route of the Camino de Santiago de Compostela shows that the corporal pain (mainly blisters and body aches) transforms into a spiritual experience that whitens the self.[12]

- The pain encountered in an obstacle race allows self-renewal as we regain consciousness of our physical body. The "electroshock therapy" obstacle from Tough Mudder is named after ECT (electroconvulsive therapy), designed to obscure the painful memories of mental health patients. For Tough Mudder participants, the 10,000-volt shock causes extreme pain and enables them to "forget everything" and escape the monotony of daily responsibilities.[13]

> Sticks and stones may break my bones,
> But chains and whips excite me
> —RIHANNA

How brands can fulfill our fantasies and imagination

Brands provide us with bridges between reality and our hopes and ideals.[14] As such, marketing appeals to our unconscious and irrational drive but often puts too much emphasis on tangible aspects of the consumption experience at the expense of daydreams and imagination.

Create and insert prompts for imaginative experiences in your marketing

The focus should not be the advertised product itself but the experience that has triggered or will trigger some imagining. Through this process, the product becomes part of the daydream or facilitates it.

Stage temporal locations

We can relive experiences from the past or daydream about experiences near and far, and these daydreams vary from mundane to elaborate wishes.

Capitalize on sensory aspects

Our daydreams might also involve sight, smell, taste, and touch. For example, the smell of fresh bread, the taste of strong coffee, and the warmth of a fire. Scents, in particular, are tied to emotions and long-term memories, yet only 3 percent of Fortune 1000 companies use scent as part of their brand experience.[15] The Mandarin Oriental, W Hotels, and Westin hotels all invested in developing their signature scent, and use scent diffusers in their HVAC systems to spread spatial fragrances in their lobbies.

> Brands are just stories that exist in our imagination. We created them to help people. Brands can't suffer and can't be happy, because they don't have a mind, they don't feel anything.
>
> Humans can suffer, and humans can be happy. So yes, you must serve your brand if that's your profession, that's your job. But in the end, make sure that it's the humans who are happy and not only the brands.
>
> —YUVAL NOAH HARARI
> HISTORIAN, PHILOSOPHER,
> AUTHOR OF SAPIENS

We also escape through daydreams . . .

A less drastic way to escape the constraints of the real world is through our daydreams. These daydreams are like our private theater where we generate stories by establishing settings, plots, characters, and even dialogues. When daydreaming, we prepare, anticipate, and organize ourselves through our imagination.

Brands and advertisements often function as simulated daydreams, mimicking the mood and emotional responses that occur in our daydreams. Brands and ads translate our fantasies and desires into everyday representations of fulfillment and illustrate the immediate satisfaction of getting what we want. Daydreaming can be mundane, at the moment, or based on similar past experiences. It can also be much more elaborate and emotionally intense.

. . . And through unusual and uncool hobbies

The global pandemic was a trauma for most of us, prompting the emergence of new lifestyles and possibilities, with people emphasizing a greater sense of personal strengths and a more profound appreciation of life. Hobbies that were once laughed at for being uncool and passé are on the rise. Champion British diver Tom Daley was seen knitting conspicuously at the Tokyo Olympic Games. In China, people are challenging the hard work culture by organizing the *Tang Ping* ("Lying Flat") movement— taking a break from overworking and being content with attainable achievements instead.[16] Hobbies have been coping mechanisms for many while locked at home during the pandemic.

Other hobbies such as cooking, baking, and gardening were a reversion to a pioneer survivalist mentality of Western settlers who needed to maintain their isolated homes. Analog hobbies soothe the worries of our modern society, such as our overreliance on technology, environmental destruction, and obsession with material gains.

Even before the pandemic, many people chose to reduce their carbon footprint, live in smaller houses, and turn to artisan hobbies like pickling, fermenting beer, beekeeping, and raising chickens. This stems from a growing desire to feel reconnected with the soil. Studies have shown these activities provide a combination of physical, cognitive, and emotional engagement that all enhance mood, creativity, and well-being.[17]

In fashion, uncool is the new cool

Footwear brands Teva and UGG have collaborated on a unique sandal that combines the rubber sole of a hiking shoe with shearling typically found on slippers or winter boots. UGGs are warm, impractical slippers for the winter. Tevas are functional sandals for the summer. Neither brand is meant to be stylish, yet they are always in style. The campaign's tagline for the hybrid footwear is "suspend your disbelief."[18] In a similar vein, furry sandals, which were initially uncool, are now a trend that can be found in high fashion collections.

Nerdy escapes

For years, "nerd" carried a negative connotation prompting the cliché of an uncool kid playing Dungeons and Dragons in the school library at lunchtime. But as internet usage exploded at the beginning of the twenty-first century, being "uncool" all of the sudden became cool. D&D keeps growing in popularity and supporting a whole industry of dice, dice trays, and other themed accessories.

Canadian-based science museum Science World is as much a tourist attraction as an educational hub. The museum deployed a campaign showcasing childhood photos of 30 notable nerds, such as primatologist

Dr. Jane Goodall, physicist Sandy Eix, and conservationist Ken Wu. Taglines for the campaigns include "the world needs more nerds," "huge nerds make a huge difference," and "giant nerd." The campaign raised more than $450,000, three times its original fundraising goal and the highest amount the museum has ever raised from a campaign. The nerd-themed merchandise caught the attention of many local celebrities, whose social media posts led to a 30 percent increase in Science World's social media engagement.[19]

KEY TAKEAWAYS

- Worried about the present and future, we find comfort in objects, places, and cultural artifacts that take us to a place that is familiar and reassuring.

- Besides physical places, we also seek a sense of permanence and reassurance in our social relationships. This explains the enduring success of *Friends*.

- We seek to step out of our skin in one way or another, a phenomenon sociologist David Le Breton called "whitening" in reference to the void suggested by the color white.

- Tattoos, cryotherapy, and obstacle course racing are examples of experiences that provide us an emotional release and freedom from the constraints of the world and our own identity.

- In the context of these experiences, pain acts as a self-shattering episode: it breaks the "weariness of the self, which is the burden of constantly having to deal with social expectations and representing oneself."

- We also escape reality through daydreams along with unusual and "uncool" hobbies.

- Brands provide us with bridges between reality and our hopes and ideals. As such, marketing appeals to our unconscious and irrational drive.

- Brands must prompt imaginative experiences, stage temporal locations, and capitalize on the sensory aspects of their products.

OUR REAL, DIGITAL, AND VIRTUAL SELVES

Technologies and platforms such as data clouds, social media, and the metaverse both facilitate and threaten our sense of self.

We wrestle with how to curate, socialize, keep, or delete vast numbers of images and other pieces of data that in many ways define who we are and who we want to appear to be.

As we interact with others in the real world, on social media, and in the metaverse, we maintain at least three versions of ourselves, possibly confusing who we really are. In the real world, we are increasingly forced to use our "real" identity. Facial recognition and other biometrics are widely used to access buildings, check our bank account balance, or unlock our phones.

Online, technology enables us to create and store a virtually unlimited amount of data, which we organize in narratives, inventing a personal myth that explains the meaning and goals of our lives through the struggles and triumphs we experience. Through these myths, we reveal how we see our past and indicate how we are likely to act in the future.

In the metaverse, we will exist through avatars that enable us to create completely new identities. Our avatars might reveal very little (if anything) about who we really are, even less so than social media does. Further, the metaverse will allow us to create numerous avatars that can constitute as many expressions of who we are and who we want to appear to be.

Permanence and abundance of personal data

One hundred and fifty years ago, only the wealthiest could have their picture taken. In the 1980s, film cartridges were only available in 12, 24, or 36 exposures, prints were expensive, and digitalization hardly existed. As a result, photographs were treasured, and taking a picture was a big deal. Professional photographers and paparazzi were seen switching between numerous camera backs so that they could shoot more than 36 pictures without having to reload.

Today, a single American might take thousands of photographs on a camera that fits in their pocket. In North America, the amount of data passing through our smartphones every month went from five gigabytes in 2017 to 11.1 gigabytes in 2020 and is projected to reach 48 gigabytes by 2026. This is largely driven by the "digital natives," a generation born with technology that allows taking and storing an infinite number of pictures. Through this digital transformation, we have lost the notion of scarcity and preciousness.

The digital-native generation

Digital natives grew up with fast internet access, smartphones, and social media. They are inherently comfortable with technology and communication tools that constitute a necessary and integral part of their daily lives. Dr. Bruce D. Perry of Baylor College of Medicine said this generation's experience with technology leads to physical changes in brain structures as a result of the new kind of stimuli created by the digital interfaces they grew up with. If anything, the thinking patterns have changed.[1]

As such, they think, learn, and understand the world around them differently from their older counterparts. Immersed in social media, this generation is much more conscious of the feedback they receive online, which affects their sense of self.

Digital natives almost systematically use social platforms to engage in friendships, self-presentation, and romantic relationships.

> ### I don't need you, I have Wi-Fi
>
> —ON A T-SHIRT WORN BY
> ONE OF MY UCLA STUDENTS

SPOTLIGHT ON | THE DELETING DATA MYTH

On February 1, 2003, the *Columbia* space shuttle blew up upon reentering the Earth's atmosphere, killing all seven astronauts and scattering debris across Texas and Louisiana. An eight-year-old, 400-megabyte hard drive was found in the debris, "burned almost beyond recognition."[2] Yet data recovery specialists at Kroll Ontrack managed to recover 99 percent of the information stored on the hard drive. Memory storage such as hard drives and memory sticks can take a lot of abuse: a BBC show host even hammered, toasted, and cremated hard drives and memory sticks, yet most of the data could still be retrieved.[3] "Deleting" a file or "wiping out" a hard drive is like removing the contents page of a book: the table of contents is gone but the chapter is still there.

The data recency bias

The amount of data produced in the world increases about 10 times every two years, suggesting that 90 percent of the world's data has been produced in the last few years. Compare how many pictures you took five years ago, three years ago, and over the last 12 months. Researchers point to a *recency bias*; most data gathered and analyzed is recent, skewing algorithms and people toward short-term findings at the expense of long-term, historical trends.[4]

Recency bias refers to the tendency of assuming that future events will resemble recent experiences. This is similar to "the availability heuristics," a tendency to base one's reasoning on what comes easily to mind. For proof that short-term analyses are misleading, take the 2009 financial crisis, which cohorts of so-called experts and leading economists failed to predict until the very last minute.[5]

We curate the pictures we keep and organize them into narratives

When scrolling through our pictures, we can easily remember all the noteworthy moments of an entire year. The abundance of pictures we take prompts us to spend more time curating, and creating narratives and memories, than ever before. When sharing pictures on social media, we participate in a social exchange in the virtual universe, putting ourselves at the center of this universe.[6] This presents an opportunity for brands to anchor themselves in memories; consumers are more loyal to brands that help people make positive memories and are entrenched in said memories.

Memories

Although they seem to be crystal clear in our minds, our memories do not exactly reflect events as we lived them. Each time we recall a memory, we accidentally alter it or diminish its accuracy.[7] We reconstruct reality and change details without even realizing it. Therefore, we increasingly rely on our smartphones for memory support, mostly by taking hundreds of pictures.

Counterintuitively, scientific studies show that taking pictures constantly actually diminishes our ability to recall our experiences, as it diverts our attention and takes us out of the moment.[8] This is because our brains can't store sensations we experience if we don't pay attention at the moment.

Cognitive offloading is the idea that we outsource our mental capabilities to computers. A study published in the journal *Science* shows that people are less likely to remember a given piece of information when they are told that this information will be saved on a computer.[9] Cognitive offloading is helpful to us when it comes to remembering mundane things such as phone numbers. But cognitive offloading becomes a tradeoff when it comes to photos: it prompts us to ask how much of our lives we want to remember purely in our brain.

Taking a picture and sharing it allows us to relive the experience with others, instead of it being kept to ourselves. Although taking photos increases our visual memories, we are more likely to ignore other stimuli around us as we take the pics.[10] When trying to snap the perfect shot, we are neither listening nor smelling nor paying attention to the moment.

Sharing photos also alters our memory. A team of researchers from NYU brought to light that when sharing pictures on social media, we become more likely to remember the experience from a third-person perspective. "If I asked you to form a picture in your mind of your Christmas experience" that you shared a photo of on social media, cognitive scientist Alexandra Barasch explains, "you'll actually start visualizing your Christmas more from an outsider's perspective."[11] In this process, taking photos becomes less enjoyable, as it makes us more self-conscious.

How our memory works

Our memory evolves as we encounter new touch points with brands, such as a review on Yelp, a friend who uses the product, and articles we read online. Further, we form associations with brands' distinctive assets, such as its logo (Apple), font, color (Tiffany's green), and shape (the Coca-Cola bottle). We hardly ever make purchasing decisions based on the product information that's available to us at the moment. Almost all our purchase decisions are driven, or at least largely influenced, by our memory.[12]

Our memory is classified into three distinct systems: stimulus, short-term memory, and long-term memory.[13]

Stimulus

This is what we receive first and is processed by our sensory memory, which stores information received from our senses.

Short-term memory

Next, iconic (visual) and echoic (auditory) stimuli pass through the short-term memory. This memory stores up to seven units of sounds or images for a short period.[14]

Long-term memory

The information that is most relevant to us is then transferred from short-term to long-term memory, where information is stored for anywhere from a few days to decades. The more we are exposed to this information, the more likely it is to become a long-term memory.

Semantic and episodic memory

Semantic memory is the memory of facts and knowledge. Semantic memory stores the words we use to describe things around us and knowledge about objects, what they mean to us and how they relate to other objects.[15] Episodic memory is the time, emotions, places, events and, generally speaking, narratives we associate with a specific object or experience.[16] Simply put, semantic memory is knowing; episodic memory is remembering. As it pertains to brands, semantic memory stores assets such as the logo, color, and tagline.[17] In contrast, episodic memory stores the affective brand interaction we experienced and the memory of the brand. Note that our semantic, episodic, sensory, short-term, and long-term memories of a brand constantly evolve as we encounter new people, usages, knowledge, and experiences. This reasoning applies just as well to any brand, be it Apple, the coffee shop next door, our local councilman, the Catholic Church, or our CEO.

Why and how to create memories

Brands must adopt and promote their distinctive brand assets, as these act as powerful mental shortcuts to help shoppers identify and find them. As exposed extensively by Byron Sharp and Jenni Romaniuk, when we can't find our brand of choice, we most likely purchase a similar alternative. It is, therefore, crucial to invest in distinctive assets, as these assets trigger the brand in the memory of the category buyer.[18] Brands can create three types of memories: Sensory memories capitalize on haptics, scents, and sounds. Semantic memories help inform and educate consumers. Episodic memories sequence the consumption experience in our minds.

Ephemerality

Ephemeral social media is defined as consuming and sharing social media content that is only available for a short time. For example, our stories on Instagram disappear after 24 hours (unless we decide to save them). Sending short, self-destructing content facilitates closeness and intimacy, two of the main reasons why these applications are so popular among younger audiences.[19] Ephemerality counterbalances our privacy concerns, whereby self-destructing data is a way to gain control.[20] In social interactions, we are often anxious from ruminating over what to say. In contrast, ephemeral messaging enables us to ruminate less and foster a form of closeness with people around us.

Ephemeral messaging is transient and grounds the interaction in the present, allowing us to feel more immersed in the activity depicted in social media stories, which increases our intent to join these activities.[21] Being in the moment frees us from elaborate thinking, allowing us to devote more energy and resources to processing and enjoying the current experience.[22] Creating ephemeral narratives allows us to convey an experience by sharing what we are doing moment by moment and offering our viewers a fleeting window into our lives. When we communicate with brands, the perceived ephemerality of text-based communication increases our feelings of trust and authenticity and, in turn, our satisfaction with the brand and its products.

In sum, brands must balance ephemeral content with permanent memories. Permanent content yields steady engagement to drive long-term brand awareness and is discoverable through search engines and social media. Temporary content gives brands a sense of urgency and drives engagements into quick, in-the-moment interactions.

> There are only two industries that call their customers "users": illegal drugs and software.
>
> —EDWARD TUFTE, PROFESSOR EMERITUS OF COMPUTER SCIENCE, POLITICAL SCIENCE, AND STATISTICS AT YALE[23]

Finstagram

Finstagram, short for "fake Instagram," refers to Instagram accounts that are kept private, with access granted to only a few followers. People open Finstagram accounts to post truer versions of themselves and off-the-cuff comments—in particular, ugly selfies, rants, private jokes, and other candid posts to a select audience. These Finstagrams capture something rarely seen on social media: reality. As people struggle to project their identity online and deal with constant feedback from their followers, more turn to Finstagrams to catch a break from being judged 24/7.

Some users set up Finstagram to create alter egos. Dominique Escandon, a student at Carnegie Mellon University, filled her Finstagram account with captions and images that portrayed her as a right-wing "trophy wife." As she puts it, "I identify very much as a feminist, and I created this character. I knew the group who followed me would understand that's not who I really was, and they would understand that it was all a joke."

In many ways, Finstagrams are an escape from an escape. When growing up, older Americans had only one self, their real-world "me," shaped by family and friends. But members of the digital-native generation can be as close to people halfway across the world online as they are with people we meet in the real world every day. Being online, however, offers the possibility of curating how we want to appear so that we showcase the best version of ourselves; our online self differs from our offline persona, affecting our perception of self. For example, if we attach our self-worth to the number of likes or views we receive, it informs the curation of our future posts. This process repeats to eventually transform us more into a brand than a person. There needs to be a realization that there will always be a difference between our online and offline selves, and social media numbers don't produce happiness or validate us as people.

The metaverse, or our third self

In virtual reality, the metaverse[24] presents us with a virtual world where we can screen external threats and completely disconnect from the real world when we decide to. Although we believe we control when we step in and out of this virtual world, the effects of the metaverse continue in some fashion after we log out, impacting our self-esteem and perception of reality.

Software developer and researcher Tony Parisi said "there is only one metaverse. It is the sum total of all publicly accessible virtual worlds, real-time 3D content, and related media that are connected on an open global network, controlled by none and accessible to all."

On social media, our real and digital personas are intertwined. Social media allows us to present a curated version of ourselves: we choose to share only specific milestones or events, such as academic accomplishments, career information, or selected pictures of parties we attend. As social media posts aren't spontaneous, we can easily enhance our image with filters, lighting, and so on. We share this information with an audience of dozens, hundreds, or even thousands of people.

In the metaverse, we exist through our "avatars" and can have multiple avatars present in the world at the same time. The metaverse is not so much about living in a fantasy world populated with dragons and unicorns; it is more about escaping the limitations of the physical world and spending time in a digital world that's an extension of real life.

Photographer Robbie Cooper traveled the world to meet the "real" people behind their avatars from online games.

> We say they're only games, these little worlds, but often
> we end up devoting more time to them than to any
> other realm of our existence until it starts to make less

sense to think of our avatars as fictional characters than as second selves.[25]

As a stepping-stone to the metaverse, brands have started to implement 3D advertising, enabling advertisers to showcase a product in 3D that users can swipe and rotate to get a better look. Of course, consumers can click a "shop now" button to purchase products from the likes of Bose, Lexus, and New Balance, a few brands that implement this format. Lancôme, Laura Mercier, and NYX have even augmented reality ads, being early adopters of a format that is projected to grow 134 percent by 2025.[26]

> Futures made of virtual insanity, now always seem
> to be governed by this love we have for
> these useless, twisting, of our new technology
> —JAMIROQUAI (1996)

Miquela Sousa

Miquela Sousa, also known as Lil Miquela, is a 20-year-old Brazilian American who garners over three million followers on Instagram and is also active on Twitter and TikTok. Miquela seems concerned with issues related to self-growth ("all I wanted for my birthday was PROGRESS [. . .] I want to know that my life is going somewhere"), identity ("identity, especially right now, is always in flux"), and societal issues ("my favorite part about this look is where we defund the police").[27]

But Miquela's life is completely invented. She is a computer-generated robot rendered so perfectly that, for two years, most followers believed she was a real person. Miquela is the creation of Brud, a Los Angeles–based start-up that administers and monetizes Miquela. Miquela is officially from

Downey, California, but could be anyone from anywhere. As such, she has "infinite potential" according to Nicole de Ayora, Brud's chief of content.

As Brud controls all aspects of Miquela's physique and personality, it makes her a perfect fit for the world she lives in. That's how Miquela believes in "a more empathetic world" and a "more tolerant future." She is also progressive in her views about race: She is "not sure [she] can comfortably identify as a woman of color" as "*Brown* was a choice made by a corporation and *woman* was an option on a computer screen." Miquela's perfect persona attracts a lot of attention and revenue. In 2018, she was named one of *Time*'s most influential people on the internet, along with Donald Trump, Kylie Jenner, and students in Parkland, Florida. She took over Prada's Instagram account as part of Milan Fashion Week that year. Miquela even has an agent, the leading talent agency CAA, and is its first digital avatar client.

In his video introduction to Meta, Mark Zuckerberg notes that the metaverse is designed around "expression," "connection," and "community" to create "an embodied experience where you're in the internet, not just looking at it." Zuckerberg illustrates his thinking by transporting his avatar to an outer space boardroom filled with other racially diverse avatars. Whether it concerns Miquela, Zuckerberg, or any of us, avatars present us with the (frightening?) opportunity to leave behind the worries and imperfections of our everyday lives to create and transform into our idealized, perfect selves.

KEY TAKEAWAYS ✸ ✸ ✸

- As we interact with others in the real world, on social media, and in the metaverse, we maintain at least three versions of ourselves, possibly confusing who we really are.

- The ease of creating and storing data such as images is both a blessing and a curse. These images enable us to create narratives to explain the meaning and goals of our lives through the struggles and triumphs we experience, but we struggle to determine and control what data should disappear and what data should be stored forever.

- Digital natives grew up with fast internet access, smartphones, and social media. They are inherently comfortable with technology and communication tools that constitute a necessary and integral part of their daily lives and can be as close to people halfway across the world online as they are with people in the real world.

- Our memories do not exactly reflect events as we lived them; each time we recall a memory, we accidentally alter it or diminish its accuracy.

- Our memory evolves as we encounter new touch points with brands, such as a review on Yelp, a friend who uses the product, and articles we read online.

- Ephemeral social media (consuming and sharing social media content that is only available for a short period) is transient and grounds the interaction in the present, allowing us to feel more immersed in the activity.

- Sending short, self-destructing content facilitates closeness and intimacy, two of the main reasons why these applications are so popular among younger audiences.

- The metaverse presents us with a virtual world where we can screen external threats and completely disconnect from the real world when we decide to.

- In the metaverse, we will likely create several avatars across multiple platforms, prompting us to create and manage multiple virtual selves.

IT'S NOT BUSINESS, IT'S PERSONAL

We are lonely in our personal lives and overwhelmed with choices as consumers.

Brand personification humanizes organizations and their products in the mind of their customers.

A brand's assemblage involves consumer emotions. Devices, social media platforms, and messaging apps are supposed to connect us to others, yet we have never felt so lonely and deprived of basic, but most important, emotions and sensations. This is particularly true of younger generations; even before the pandemic, 22 percent of millennials reported having no friends at all. During the pandemic, a survey found that 71 percent of millennials and almost 79 percent of Gen Z respondents felt lonely.[1]

Brands can foster more meaningful relationships with their customers by being more empathetic and delivering a personalized experience, such as personalized virtual beauty consultations from a skincare brand. To do so, brands must collect, analyze, and leverage data about our demographics, psychographics, personality traits, behavior, and attitudes to deliver personalized recommendations.

This points to the ambivalence of giving up some privacy in return for more personalized and relevant products and consumption experiences.

Algorithms and their limitations

Algorithms are meant to help organize and extract insights from big data sets. They allow for scale and automation, which in turn enables cost efficiencies. Further, artificial intelligence can train algorithms over time, allowing said algorithms to predict future consumer trends and needs.

This element—high volume, extremely varied, and traveling at some velocity—is commonly referred to as "big data."

In the marketing and market research arenas, big data strategies are often expected to enable automated, scalable, and cost-efficient analytics, but making sense of this data is easier said than done. An example of this is the recent failure of Zillow Offers. This algorithm was supposed to enable Zillow to accurately predict swings in home prices and buy houses at the best possible price, make minor renovations, and then sell these houses quickly and profitably. In reality, the value of a property is largely driven by the neighborhood, the cachet of the home, and its history, to name a few parameters an algorithm can't factor in. Ultimately, Zillow Offers shut down, leading to a $569 million loss and the termination of two thousand employees.[2]

Zillow Offers failed mostly because it implemented a top-down approach to data analysis, whereby machines spot size-specific dimensions or concepts in the data, bringing to light what is already in existence.

Our ambivalent attitude

More than two billion people use Facebook Messenger, Google Assistant, and Amazon Echo, allowing brands to communicate directly with them and serve personalized content and offerings. Technically, the data each user provides through this software and hardware can easily be combined with their search and browsing history, media consumption, email information, in-home security, geolocation data, and even facial recognition. The realm of data that tech brands collect keeps expanding: TikTok recently updated its privacy policy to disclose that it "may collect biometric identifiers and biometric information" from user content. This includes things like "faceprints and voiceprints."[3]

Amid these trends, people are becoming increasingly comfortable sharing their data; nearly half of users will happily give their information away in return for personalized services and products—a 7 percent rise since 2013.[4] Millennials and members of Gen Z are even more inclined than other age cohorts (over 50 percent) to share their data with tech brands, as they are more exposed to the benefits through curated content on various platforms.

Where is our data going?

Despite this comfort, people have become increasingly concerned and mindful of how tech companies collect, analyze, and monetize their data. A recent Ipsos study reveals that 66 percent of people are more concerned about privacy and security, and 57 percent feel they need to learn more about ways to protect themselves.

Data usage is also increasingly regulated through legislation. Laws bring some transparency into what data is being collected and stored and empower users to control how their data is being used. For example, Article 17 of the UK GDPR gives individuals the right to have their data erased. This is also known as the "right to be forgotten." Brands must therefore reassure users on how their data is used, as 71 percent of consumers would stop doing business with a company if it gave away sensitive information without permission.

How brands can monetize data for years to come

People will share an exponential amount of personal data with tech brands across an increasingly wide and diverse range of devices and platforms. Brands can continue to further monetize data as long as they provide their users with tangible benefits and reassure them that their practices are transparent and ethical.

Here are some guidelines to help brands collect and monetize for years to come:

- Education: Brands must educate the public on how they collect, analyze, monetize, and store data, and how these actions benefit users.

- Data sovereignty: Tech-centric terminology such as "cloud computing" and "algorithm" sound elusive to most people and trigger anxiety for some. Brands can reassure the public by showing them where their data is stored, preferably in their users' country of residence.

- Credibility: With its "Azure Government Top Secret" service, Microsoft demonstrates its ability to handle sensitive information on behalf of government agencies. In a similar vein, messaging services like Telegram and Signal promise to encode users' messages.

- Data preservation: Many data sets are important and precious for the future of humanity, like gene sequences, knowledge of geography and physics, and demographic data. Tech brands can help government agencies, scientists, and academics store and organize this data, and help keep the world's knowledge safe and secure.

How we communicate with people and brands

When the global pandemic restricted in-person interactions, people across all age groups learned to rely heavily on technology to communicate with others. They now expect their communications with brands to be just as seamless and timely.

Brands must evolve the way they communicate with customers

People expect to communicate with brands as fast and seamlessly as they do with their friends, family, and associates. Brands must accelerate their digital transformation to communicate with customers through one-on-one interactions while handling a large volume of contacts in a cost- and time-efficient fashion to foster strong, long-lasting relationships. Technologies such as messaging, chatbots, and AI can enable brands to deliver this personal customer experience. AI-powered chatbots, in particular, help practitioners streamline their customers' journeys and cut costs. These chatbots save brands $0.70 per customer interaction and can answer up to 80 percent of routine questions.[5] In addition, retail chatbots deliver a personalized experience for every customer and can help raise shopping cart conversion rates by up to 30 percent.

Laying the groundwork for meaningful customer relationships

The customer journey is increasingly complex: Brands need to support their customers effectively across all touch points, as people who shop across multiple channels spend three times more than single-channel shoppers. Furthermore, shoppers are becoming wary of generic marketing communication and would rather engage in a more personal relationship with brands.[6]

Brands and their marketing must support who we really are

Our identities have several demographic components that shape our needs as individuals and as consumers. For example, males tend to purchase hair care and grooming products that are designed specifically for the male gender. Men, in particular, have become keen on making their own choices; 26 percent would purchase skincare products for themselves in the future, 42 percent would buy their own cosmetics, and 46 percent their own clothing items.

Although many marketers still assume that marketing to men requires stereotypical depictions of beauty, younger men are increasingly open to more diverse standards. In a study for the Unstereotype Alliance,[7] Ipsos asked men about two ads that both showcased unconventional beauty. The first advertisement, for Dove, depicted a curvy young lady with pink and blue hair and tattoos. The second ad, for underwear garment brand Knix, showed 13 women all with skin tones and body shapes of many sorts. The results of this study are unequivocal: Many younger men (63 percent) said the Dove ad made them feel good about the brand, versus 33 percent of older men. For the Knix ad, 41 percent of younger men agreed with this same statement, versus 18 percent of older men.

Women also want to see advertisers deliver more authenticity. When portraying people in advertising, 56 percent of women would like ads to show a man cooking or doing household chores, 55 percent depicting an older woman as attractive, and 50 percent portraying women as decisive and accomplished.[8] Conversely, nearly half of women surveyed (46 percent) would like to see fewer ads that depict beautiful women as young women and men as decision makers (36 percent).

In response to this longing for authentic beauty, leading ad agency Ogilvy UK no longer works with influencers who edit their bodies and faces for ads. Ogilvy recognizes they "have a duty of care as marketers, as agencies and brands to the next generation of people so they don't grow up with the same stuff we are seeing now,"[9] says Rahul Titus, Ogilvy's head of influence. Titus knows it will take time for the rest of the industry to follow suit.

Omsom

Omsom is a Vietnamese phrase that means noisy, rambunctious, and riotous. Co-founders Kim and Vanessa Pham founded Omsom to bring "loud and proud" Asian flavors to the everyday cook and to become the authority in Asian foods in CPG.[10] Its vision is to celebrate Asian communities while being a staple in all American pantries, and Omsom's marketing is quirky and its packaging design is rather loud. That's the founders' way to tell the stories about who they are and their values through a genuine, "no-BS" narrative.[11] Omsom is the story of two sisters born from Vietnamese refugees. The brand even enlisted their dad for a series on social media called "Papa Pham Reacts," who voices his take on his daughter's endeavors.

Omsom was created in response to Asian products that were "diluted and bastardized," most often representing Asian culture through stereotypical branding centered on dragons, pandas, and bamboos. Omsom's "community" (a.k.a. target audience) is primarily Asian Americans who grew up on Asian flavors but don't have the time or skills to cook from scratch.

Omsom guides its brand narrative, for example, when it created a seven-slide deck to explain why it did not use the word *authenticity* to describe Omsom. Calling for authenticity in food is a burden and prompts specific ideas around how the food should taste, look, and cost. The deck is a way for the brand "to create space for an honest dialogue and connect with the broader community."[12] Launched during the pandemic, the company's cooking kits have sold out three times and accrued a 2,000-strong wait list.

The changing dynamic of e-commerce and direct-to-consumer relationships

The global pandemic has greatly accelerated the consumer shift to online shopping. In the United States, e-commerce penetration increased as much in the first half of 2020 as it did over the prior decade. In Europe, the COVID-19 crisis raised overall digital adoption from 81 percent to 95 percent.[13] In the meantime, the demise of the third-party cookie and stringent legal regulations (GDPR, CCPA) forced brands to double down on their efforts to collect, analyze, and monetize first-party data. These changing consumer behaviors and new legal restrictions have prompted brands to accelerate their digital transformation and deliver a seamless omnichannel shopping experience.

Further, this new market environment changes the dynamic between big legacy brands, digital-native brands, traditional retailers, and e-commerce platforms. It is 1,000 times cheaper to launch a tech start-up today than 20 years ago,[14] and even the smallest brands can open and advertise a storefront in a few clicks. On the other hand, the cost of acquiring new customers keeps rising and many DTCs/e-commerce brands struggle to retain their subscribers. Therefore, digital-native brands increasingly lean on brick-and-mortar stores to reach large audiences and achieve sales volumes that only traditional retail can offer.

We now favor DTC and e-commerce across all categories

An Ipsos Fast Facts study on US consumers' online and offline shopping habits reveals that consumers' positive sentiments toward DTC and e-commerce retailers are pretty much on par with traditional stores.

Which best describes how you feel about the following types of retailers?
Sample Base=989/1303/1424

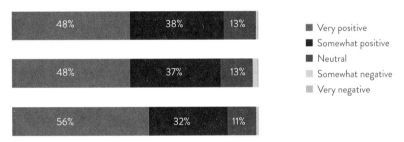

Shoppers now turn to e-commerce for furnishing, groceries, and automotive—categories that until recently were exclusive to brick-and-mortar retailers. This presents new challenges for brands. While digital-native brands need to grow sustainably and exponentially, legacy brands need to harness the power of DTC and e-commerce to foster a personal and seamless relationship with their customers.

Many direct-to-consumer brands swirl in a sea of sameness

Since the creation of eyewear maker Warby Parker in 2010 and Dollar Shave Club (razors and grooming products) in 2011, over 400 DTC brands have launched,[15] mostly in clothing and apparel (Bonobos, UNTUCKit), pet care (BarkBox, The Farmer's Dog), home and furnishing (Casper, Parachute), and even wealth management (Robinhood, Lemonade).

The original recipe for success seemed simple enough: a limited assortment of products focused on one narrow category available at a better price. Ten years on, building and growing a digital-first brand proves to be as challenging as with any other brand.

DTC brands struggle to differentiate

While DTC brands often claim to be disruptive and challengers in their respective arenas, their identity and tone of voice are often similar. The same goes for their brand promise of "cutting out the middleman" (Brooklinen, Mejuri, Brilliant), positioning themselves as "underdogs" (Oscar, Monica + Andy), and being "different" from all other companies (Burrow, Harry's, Solé).

Funneling traffic to a merchant website is expensive and cumbersome

DTC increasingly relies on dedicated marketplaces like The Fascination to offset the cost of digital advertising. On these portals, visitors can discover, learn about, and eventually shop from hundreds of digitally-native brands like Allbirds, UNTUCKit, and S'well in one place.

Brick-and-mortar retail and digital-native brands can establish mutually beneficial relationships

As online shopping, in general, is becoming more competitive, the cost of digital advertising has soared, resulting in a steep increase in customer acquisition costs. Also, most digital-first brands only appeal to narrow online audiences. Aware that brick-and-mortar retail still accounts for about 85 percent of the US retail market,[16] digital-first brands turn to traditional retailers to reach mass audiences and drive greater sales volume.

That's how brands like Caraway Home partnered with Crate & Barrel when its online growth plateaued. Other brands like Harry's (shaving products), Quip (oral care), and Native (personal care) now sell their products at Target.

Facing competition, Netflix, which boasts 200 million subscribers, needs to build its retail presence, starting with a digital storefront on Walmart's website to sell merchandise for its blockbuster shows like *Squid Game* and *The Crown*.[17]

Traditional brands are shifting to a DTC model

DTC also presents existing brands with expansion opportunities. In 2010, DTC accounted for only 15 percent of Nike's total revenue, but by 2021, the athletics brand has grown its DTC business to $44.5 billion, or 40 percent of its revenue. Moving forward, Nike plans on stepping farther back from wholesalers to focus on its stores and digital channels.[18] The same goes for Adidas, which plans to reach a 50 percent DTC business by 2025, hoping this channel will drive 80 percent or more of the company's net sales growth.[19]

DTC sales come with lower margins before taxes than wholesale sales, and sales volume tends to be a lot lower,[20] but DTC sales are growing much faster than wholesale and enable brands to fully control marketing and customer experience while accumulating data about their customers. To make sense of this data, brands will increasingly invest in AI and analytical capabilities. Nike has recently acquired three data analytics companies: Celect (predictive analytics), Zodiac (demand sensing), and Datalogue (machine learning).

These capabilities allow Nike to anticipate demand and redistribute products, personalize recommendations, and use push marketing to manage lifetime value. It also leverages sentiment analysis to create new products and services, such as Nike Training Club.

The temptation to focus on tactical metrics and the imperative for brand strategy

The average CMO tenure as of 2020 is only 40 months, the lowest since 2009. The median tenure for the same function is 25.5 months, down from 30 months in 2019.[21] Beyond the C-suite, the tenure of marketers at all levels keeps shrinking. And the post-pandemic booming employment market has led to a phenomenon coined "The Great Resignation," where workers and executives are resigning in droves for better opportunities.

Marketers at all levels are often goal-set toward quarterly or even monthly objectives and are keen on making a quick impact to tout their achievements to prospective employers. Therefore, they often prioritize short-term marketing tactics that drive clicks and purchases at the expense of long-term brand-building efforts.

However, e-commerce brands will still need to build a consistent identity and set of associations to make them easily recognizable and an automatic choice, especially as DTC channels become more saturated. The failure of the e-commerce company Brandless, which promised to focus on products and abandon branding, shows that consumers favor trusted brands over unbranded, functional products.

The three pillars for building a digital-first brand

1. First-party data collection

The exponential advantage of digital-native brands over traditional companies is the first-party data they own on their users, enabling these brands to own the entire consumer journey, from awareness through sales and retention. As data privacy regulations become more stringent and third-party cookies are phased out, first-party data will become more valuable to uncover new trends, develop new products, and measure marketing performance. Ipsos creates and manages consumer communities that enable brands to access on-tap audiences through video interviews, live chats, discussion boards, blogs, diaries, and surveys. Through these communities, Ipsos fosters a social and collaborative customer-brand experience that yields authentic discovery and insights.

2. Combine, analyze, and monetize disparate data sets

Marketers that adopt a digital-first strategy can grow brand awareness and preference, and the desired set of associations' sales performance no longer comes at the expense of brand equity and vice versa.

To deliver on this promise, data engineers must combine disparate data sets that include customer sales data, surveys, advertising exposure and engagement measures, social media, search data, and macro-economic and societal data.

Next, data scientists must leverage natural language processing, natural language understanding, and apply artificial intelligence to model time-series data to sort the signal from the noise, infer connections between these different data sources, find the short-term signals of long-term brand growth, and ultimately help predict, measure, and optimize marketing performance and long-term brand growth.

3. Market at the moment of need

Based on these dynamics, scalable models, and intuitive reporting tools, marketers can target specific audience segments based on their demographics, psychographics, and purchase history. They can design audiences based on

- Life stages and need states/moments of needs

- Behavioral surrogates for category needs and motivations
- Past category and brand interest
- Sequencing the consumer journey

The unboxing experience

Unboxing pictures and videos are popular on social media, translating into free advertising for brands. The hashtag #unboxing returns over 700,000 posts on Instagram, while a search for *unboxing* on YouTube delivers over 90 million results.

Dr. Pamela Rutledge of the Media Psychology Center unpacked (pun intended) the reasons why we are drawn to unboxing. First, it cultivates *anticipation and intrigue*, whereby our brand speculates what might or might not be in the box. Next, the *reveal* acts as a payoff; we feel rewarded from seeing what's inside the box and how it aligns with what we expected.

Unboxing videos can be considered narratives, with the person breaking through the fourth wall (the barrier between the performer and his audience) and making the viewer part of the story. "Even though you rationally know [the] person in that video does not see you and that they taped it at some other time, part of your brain responds to it as if it was a normal social situation," notes Rutledge.[22]

As trivial as they may seem, these videos are a powerful means for brands to advertise their products. People watch unboxing videos when researching product alternatives before buying and are more likely to buy after watching a product video. And finally, because these videos are shot by customers, they cost nothing to brands.

The unboxing experience is particularly important to brands as the pandemic has permanently limited the time we spend in stores. Also, unboxing is a sensory experience that provides us with the opportunity to feel, touch, hear, see, and smell the brand. Further, brands that sell online and deliver at home control the entire shopping journey, from the website to the moment the product is received and unboxed.

How to deliver a compelling unboxing experience

As the last stage in the shopping journey, unboxing impacts customers' perceptions of the entire experience with the brand and is the last thing they will remember. Here are some guidelines on designing a memorable unboxing experience:

- Design packaging that is easy to read, open, and use so that all consumers, including ones with disabilities, will be able to unpack the product easily and pleasantly.

- Build anticipation with package tracking updates.

- Personalize the experience by adding the customer's name and acknowledging a prior order.

- Align the unboxing experience with your brand values. For example, use packaging that is recyclable if your brand narrative is about sustainability.

- Leverage the unboxing experience to cross-sell and upsell other products. For example, add QR codes that guide consumers to a microsite with content that illustrates how to use the product, information on the product itself, and discounts toward companion products.

KEY TAKEAWAYS

- Brands can foster meaningful relationships with their customers by being more empathetic and delivering a personalized experience.
- Brands collect, organize, and monetize data about our behaviors and attitudes, prompting us to feel ambivalent about giving up some privacy in return for more personalized and relevant products and consumption experiences.
- Ultimately, brands can continue to further monetize data as long as they provide their users with tangible benefits and reassure them that their practices are transparent and ethical.
- The global pandemic has accelerated the consumer shift to online shopping. Brands must accelerate their digital transformation and deliver a seamless omnichannel shopping experience.
- Traditional retail brands need to learn from direct-to-consumer brands that leverage data and algorithms as the foundation for delivering a personalized customer experience.
- Direct-to-consumer brands need to leverage the store footprint of these retailers to access wider audiences and establish a physical presence.
- Unboxing pictures and videos, an increasingly popular trend on social media, translates into free advertising for brands.

- Unboxing videos can be considered as narratives that people share, with the person unboxing breaking through the fourth wall (the barrier between the performer and his audience) and making the viewer part of the story.

- The unboxing experience has become particularly important to brands as the pandemic has permanently limited the time we spend in stores.

PART
2 | HOW
BRANDS
CAN
TRANSFORM
MY WORLD

PERCEPTION
IS THE TRUTH

We construct our own truths based on our perception of the world, the information we are exposed to, and, in a way, what we want the truth to be.

In marketing, what matters is how people perceive the brand, not what the brand and product really are.

The things that seem true and universal are, in fact, just our own unique experiences of the world. Our perception of the world is not only determined by sensory input, but other factors such as feelings, physical ability, and energy level.

If you are overweight or tired, for example, distances look farther. That's why Disney parks are designed using "forced perspective," which enables Disney's "Imagineers" to make objects look taller than they are and manipulate the perceived distance between objects. On Main Street, guests entering the park instantly notice the Sleeping Beauty castle looming at the end of a seemingly long street. However, this same street seems shorter when guests leave the park in the opposite direction. That's because buildings on Main Street are designed so that the side closer to the gate comes down at a wider angle than the side closer to the castle. These differences in consumer perception affect how elements are brought together in brand assemblages. Here's how.

Creating customer perception

Whether we are visiting a theme park, buying a car, or choosing a tube of toothpaste, perception determines how much value we attribute to products and services. Most of the time, the facts have little to no importance.

Perhaps the best illustration of this is our choice of political candidates. I was living in Chicago in 2008 when then-senator Barack Obama ran for president for the first time. Obama's campaign was a well-oiled marketing machine, complete with social media targeting (a very novel concept at the time), the distinctive "Rising Sun" logo, and empowering taglines such as "Yes, we can" and "Change we can believe in." People traveled hundreds of miles to attend his meetings and chant these taglines, dressed in campaign gear from head to toe. But when attendees were asked after a rally to name the three measures Obama was campaigning for, most couldn't answer.

Facts do not have much to do with who is electable. What is most important is to know that a large group of people like you already supports the candidate (not unlike McDonald's "billions and billions served"). As psychologist Drew Westen from Emory University puts it, "Two-thirds of voters' decisions to support one candidate or another could be accounted for by two simple variables: their partisan feelings and their feelings toward the candidates. Candidates' positions on the issues had only a modest effect on their electoral preferences."[1] That's why most political ads focus on the tribe that already supports the candidate (the candidate is a hero for the good people like us), rather than why we should support the candidate.

As consumers, we take most marketers' information at face value because we don't have the expertise, time, or, frankly, the motivation to challenge what marketing claims to be true. Granted, many of these claims are regulated by government agencies and legislative officials. I am not suggesting all these claims are fraudulent, just that most of the time we have to take them at face value. Consider these examples:

- Supersmile Extra White toothpaste claims its product is "Clinically proven to whiten nine shades in 30 days (on average), leaving you with a smile that sparkles like the 20-carat diamond you are."[2] Inquisitive consumers, beware: The claim is only substantiated by a 30-day clinical trial that compares groups of users to nonusers.

- "Fifteen minutes could save you 15 percent or more on car insurance." Note that the ad says Geico *could* save us 15 percent, not that it *will*. The reality is even if Geico rates can be almost 20 percent cheaper than the median rate, they are not always the cheapest.

Brands change our perception of reality

When it comes to the assemblages that contribute to different products, in many cases, few people—not even the product owners—could differentiate and choose certain products if it wasn't for the brand. In a blind test, we would be hard-pressed to recognize Grey Goose Vodka from Tito's or Ketel One. Plus, the temperature of the glass, the glass itself, and the ice cubes all alter the flavor. What we buy is not so much the taste but how the brand makes us feel:

- Grey Goose is about living "victoriously," enabling its consumers to indulge in a genuine, relatable luxury.[3]

- Tito's conveys southern conviviality, love of music, and the free-spirited attitude typical of Austin, where it was founded.

- Ketel One aims to appeal to mindful drinkers that seek a premium, organic, and natural beverage for a night in with friends.[4]

This same reasoning applies to other product categories like bleach (think of Clorox vs. Walmart's Great Value), beer (Coors Light vs. Miller Light vs. Bud Light), water (Dasani vs. Evian vs. Smartwater), and over-the-counter medicine (Advil, Motrin, and CVS Health, which all carry the same active ingredient, ibuprofen).

Less expensive brands often deliver better products than name brands. Costco's Kirkland Olive Oil performed better in blind tests than the likes of O California, Filippo Berio, and Lucini, which are all twice as expensive. An even more blatant example of the power of branding is UK's cell phone carrier Virgin Mobile. In the early 2000s, users rated Virgin more than 10 percent superior to T-Mobile on attributes like signal clarity and call reliability.[5] At the time, Virgin Mobile was renting all of its mobile network from T-Mobile. Virgin's perceived superiority was therefore based solely on the strength of its brand.

Cognitive fluency and false memories

A brand's assemblages also involve judgments. Every day, we make judgments and decisions about people and brands based on the way they present themselves. Given the many options available, we prefer things that are easy to think about and remember rather than the difficult ones. This feeling of ease or difficulty is known as *cognitive fluency*.

For example, food ingredients like methylcellulose, butylated hydroxy anisole, and potassium benzoate sound complicated and hence scary. The disfluency of these names makes these ingredients more foreign and, therefore, riskier to eat. In contrast, KIND Snacks makes its products only with ingredients we can see and pronounce. Its snacks are simply named: "Dark Chocolate Nuts & Sea Salts," "Peanut Butter Dark Chocolate," and "Cranberry Almond."

Other aspects of information presentation that seem insignificant have a surprisingly strong impact on people's perceptions and behavior. Cognitive fluency is subtle and pervasive; research shows that a statement printed in a darker color will be perceived as more truthful than the same statement printed in a lighter color with less background contrast because it's easier to decipher—subconsciously assuming it is familiar and therefore true.[6]

Familiarity is one of the strongest drivers of our behavior because familiar things don't require as much mental processing as things that are new and different. Familiar things are attractive because they require minimal resources and feel easy to understand. It is, therefore, often used as a mental shortcut to determine whether the stimulus is something we encountered before.[7]

> **A reliable way to make people believe in falsehoods**
> **is frequent repetition, because familiarity is not**
> **easily distinguished from the truth.**
>
> —NOBEL PRIZE WINNER AND PSYCHOLOGIST DANIEL
> KAHNEMAN IN *THINKING, FAST AND SLOW*

More on false memories

False memories are recollections that seem real but are fabricated or distorted recollections of events. For example, we might leave the house thinking we started the dishwasher only to come home and find we didn't. In the bigger scheme of things, memories of past events are often reconstructed as we age or as our worldview changes.

In advertising, exposure to vivid commercials tricks the hippocampus (center of long-term memory embedded into the temporal lobe of the brain) into believing that what we see in the ad happened to us.[8] In an experiment, 100 participants were introduced to a fictitious product called "Orville Redenbacher's Gourmet Fresh Microwave Popcorn." Then, some participants were assigned to watch a low-imagery text ad that described the taste of the popcorn. Other participants watched a high-imagery commercial featuring happy, enthusiastic people enjoying the popcorn in their living room. A week later, participants were quizzed about their memory of the product.

People who saw the low-imagery ad were unlikely to report having tried the snack food, while people who watched the vivid commercial were more likely to say they had tried the popcorn and rated the product favorably. Priyali Rajagopal and Nicole Montgomery, the lead authors of the paper, noted that "viewing the vivid advertisement created a false memory of eating the popcorn, despite the fact that eating the non-existent product would have been impossible."[9]

Alternative facts

We tend to believe and share evidence that reinforces our views and reject anything that contradicts them. Former president Donald Trump's adviser Kellyanne Conway knew this when, in January 2017, she coined the term "alternative facts." During a *Meet the Press* interview,[10] Conway defended White House Press Secretary Sean Spicer's false statement about how many people attended Trump's inauguration. Her main strategy relied on the public's low opinion of mainstream journalism, creating an opening for an alternate version of reality, no matter its level of accuracy.

Jay Van Bavel is an associate professor of psychology and neural science who researches how political beliefs and group identities shape the mind and brain. "When you have a really strong commitment to a group or belief and you get information that contradicts what you already know, you construct new ways of thinking about that information rather than updating your belief."[11] In line with this reasoning, psychologist Leon Festinger infiltrated a cult that predicted the destruction of the world.[12] Rather than abandoning the cult on the day the prediction didn't come true, followers doubled down on their belief instead, proselytizing even more frequently.

As with many other things, social media has put "alternative facts" on steroids. Platforms such as Facebook enable us to share our views with thousands—potentially millions—in seconds. Further, social media platforms' algorithms are designed to identify and subsequently serve a uniquely crafted version of reality that is more sensational than reality to keep our attention, which these companies monetize.

> Our penchant for fluency makes us susceptible to
> bullshit—if it feels right, it is right—and when that
> vulnerability is scaled up to the level of media, you
> get truthiness and fake news.
>
> —DENNIS PROFFITT AND DRAKE BAER IN
> *PERCEPTION: HOW OUR BODIES SHAPE OUR MINDS*

SPOTLIGHT ON | THE TRUMP BRAND

All politics aside, former president Trump has built one of the most recognizable brands in the world. Tax documents show that Trump's finances were in great distress in early 2004 after he squandered the $423 million inheritance he received from his father.[13] On the verge of bankruptcy, *The Apprentice* TV show made Trump a household name, bolstering his personal myth as a successful businessman.[14] As outrageous as it may seem, this justified spending $70,000 on hairstyling expenses during his time on the show: Trump was simply treating his hair as the most salient attribute of his brand.[15] With no political experience and few, if any, political connections, one can largely credit Trump's personal brand for helping him secure the GOP nomination. Over time, the Trump brand, once valued at more than $4 billion, has become polarizing. With that said, Trump still earns income from countless licensing deals around the world where real estate promoters pay to put his name on the buildings they operate. In the meantime, revenues from Trump's most important golf and hospitality assets have plummeted after being greatly affected by the pandemic.[16]

SPOTLIGHT ON | THE MICHELIN GUIDE

In many categories, rankings are based on the subjective evaluation of small groups of so-called experts who often keep their evaluation criteria under wraps. At times, these secret, arbitrary evaluation criteria come under scrutiny.[17] One example is the *Michelin Guide*, which bestows one, two, or three stars on the best restaurants in countries where the guide is published. Earning (and then keeping) stars is the work of a lifetime for chefs, with three stars being the ultimate distinction. Since its launch in the early twentieth century, the guide has shaped the reputation of restaurants, sometimes with tragic consequences; the suicide of Chef

Bernard Loiseau in 2003 was linked by some to rumors that the *Michelin Guide* was about to lower his star rating. Ten years later, the suicide of Benoît Violier also came under scrutiny after the chef spoke openly about the stress and perfectionism needed to maintain his three stars.[18]

According to a former inspector, the guide employs only five people to inspect the 10,000-plus restaurants that are theoretically up for review every year. Also, some top-tier restaurants are secretly deemed "untouchable" and will always keep their three stars, even though some of them no longer meet the guide's supposedly stringent criteria.[19]

For some chefs, the guide's questionable ranking process, extensive financial investments needed to earn and maintain stars, and stress are not worth it. Many chefs, including Marco Pierre White in the UK, Julio Bosca in Spain, and Michel Bras in France, "returned" their stars, a process that is only symbolic as stars are not awarded to the chefs but to their restaurants.

How brands can create a Reason to Believe

A key part of a brand's assemblages is a "Reason to Believe" (RTB). At the most basic level, the RTB is why your customer should believe you. RTB is about gaining a unique position in someone's mind and heart. What makes our claims and promises credible and trustworthy? Here are some examples:

Awards and accreditations

- The *Michelin Guide* and James Beard Award for restaurants (despite the controversies above)

- *The New York Times* and *Wall Street Journal* bestseller lists for books

- The Oscars for motion pictures

As these accolades are hard to secure, you may enter lesser-known contests just to be able to claim that your product, book, or movie is "award-winning."

Category expertise and longevity

These include being "a market leader" and/or operating for "100 years." Note that either claim can be hard to vet.

Dress the part

Store associates at Kiehl's Cosmetics wear white coats, instantly conveying the store's apothecary narrative.

Although Kiehl's started as an old-world apothecary in New York City's East Village in 1851, global beauty conglomerate L'Oréal purchased the brand in 2000. Its Creme de Corps, for example, is made in New Jersey; none of the products are compounded in store.

Reviews and testimonials

People like people similar to themselves and trust those who validate the quality of a product or service they bought with their hard-earned cash. Reviews for "ordinary" people have more credence than celebrities, models in advertisements, brand spokespersons, or anyone else who has a vested interest in the brand's success.

Aesthetic consumerism: We shape reality through our camera lens

In an increasingly virtual world, we feel more rewarded with aesthetic experiences that embrace all forms of sensory experiences related to paintings, music, and the arts.[20] It includes sensory experiences derived from everyday objects.[21] Finally, aesthetics refers to symbolism, imagery, beauty, taste, and feelings.[22]

> **It is common for those who have glimpsed something beautiful to express regret at not having been able to photograph it. So successful has been the camera's role in beautifying the world that photographs, rather than the world, have become the standard of the beautiful.**
>
> —SUSAN SONTAG[23]

Photographs are instant antiques. Just like the artificial ruin in romantic architecture, the ruin is created to be suggestive of the past and deepen the historical aspect of a landscape.

The aesthetic-usability effect

The aesthetic-usability effect refers to a phenomenon in which consumers perceive a product with a more aesthetic design as easier to use than a product with a less aesthetic design. In general, aesthetic designs seem easier to use and are more likely to be used, whether or not they are actually easier. People are also more likely to develop positive feelings toward a product that is aesthetically pleasing, such as loyalty, patience, and affection. As such, aesthetics should not be only about style and beauty but also the relationship between the product and the user and the way the product shapes relationships between humans and the world around them. For example, leaving an object unfinished gives the object owner a role in continuing the story. Like the first part of an unfinished sentence, it starts a conversation with the user that he can pick up and continue. This storytelling with objects promotes belonging and connection. Think of torn jeans or ones with patches: their wear-out is integrated into the overall design. In this process, ephemerality becomes a key component of the object.

What magicians can teach us about branding

> **The secret of showmanship consists not of what you really do, but what the mystery-loving public thinks you do.**
>
> —HARRY HOUDINI

Harry Houdini is arguably the world's best-known magician, although his brother, The Great Hardeen, was a better magician and escape artist. Houdini was a better showman and had more presence and star power; Houdini and Hardeen even pretended to feud over who was a better magician—a sibling rivalry was a story no media outlet could turn down. The staged feud generated media attention for many years.

On stage, Houdini developed his image by telling stories to his audience about his shows, his escapes, and himself. Houdini carefully constructed a perception of being someone larger than life, constantly defying death, performing greater escapes, and ultimately coming out on top in a spectacular way.

Just like marketers who often stage their products in utopian worlds, magicians present a world in which the laws of nature are suspended.[24] Here are some tips marketers can learn from magicians:

- Work on planning and mastering a process to persuade their audience with an impressive outcome.

- Create illusory worlds of beauty and magic.

- Magic, just like many brands, is intrinsically associated with illusion, enthusiasm, and surprise.

- It is all about showmanship. Magicians can use old tricks as long as they are seamlessly executed and presented in a new way. Catching a bullet, making objects disappear, or seeing someone levitating all involve the suspension of disbelief.

- To be effective, marketing must be engaging for the audience. The product in and of itself hardly ever does the trick.

Mastering techniques to make the result look effortless

Magicians spend hours learning and perfecting dexterity to create the illusion of magic. An amateur magician will need to spend at least fifty hours studying enough tricks to entertain family and friends for fifteen to twenty minutes.[25] Professional magicians never stop practicing.

Orchestrate perceptual clues

In magic and marketing, our minds make inferences based on certain perpetual clues. A magician leads us to believe he can cut someone in half and restore them. Magic is about distorting someone's reality and showing them something impossible. Marketing leads us to believe that Axe deodorant will make us more attractive and desirable to potential mates.

Manage your audience's attention

When watching a magic show, spectators only focus on the narrative aspect of the performance. In magic, this is mostly referred to as *misdirection*. In marketing, this is *attention management*, ensuring that consumers will remember the advertisement for a specific product.

Entertain

Shops, restaurants, websites, and apps are staged to create a universe that will carry the consumer away from reality. Clothes on the rack get delivered in cardboard boxes, most tomatoes served on pizzas are canned, and e-commerce platforms are, by definition, lines of codes.

Remain silent

"If you are smart enough to work silently, it brings a huge amount of wonder," says American magician Penn Jillette. His partner, Teller, notes, "When you don't talk, the audience has to tell itself the story and they don't know where it is going."

KEY TAKEAWAYS ✳ ✳ ✳

- The things that seem true and universal are just our own unique experiences of the world.

- Disney exemplifies the power of brand perception: when designing amusement parks, Disney's "Imagineers" make objects look taller than they are and manipulate the perceived distance between objects.

- The importance of perception is exacerbated in politics: two-thirds of voters' decisions are based on their partisan feelings toward the candidate.

- Almost no one, not even the product owners, could differentiate certain products like vodka, beer, or bleach if it wasn't for the brand label.

- Often, less expensive brands perform much better than name brands in blind tests.

- Given the myriad of options available to us, we prefer things that are easy to think about and remember rather than difficult ones. This feeling of ease or difficulty is known as *cognitive fluency*.

- False memories are recollections that seem real but are fabricated or distorted. For example, we might leave the house thinking we started the dishwasher, only to come home and find out we didn't.

- Our convictions shape the kind of evidence we accept, rather than the other way around. We tend to believe and share evidence that reinforces our views but reject anything that contradicts them.

- The Reason to Believe (RTB) is why your customer should believe you. RTB is about gaining a unique position in someone's mind and heart.

- In an increasingly virtual world, we seek and feel more rewarded with sensory experiences. Aesthetics embrace all forms of sensory experiences related to paintings, music, and the arts.

- Brands, objects, and products help satisfy the aesthetic needs of consumers through sensory experiences.

- Aesthetics should be not only about style and beauty but also the relationship between the product and the user and the way the product shapes relationships between humans and the world around them.

- Obsolescence is most often perceived or aesthetic. Brands implement a small aesthetic change, which rarely, if ever, improves functionality.

THE REMIX ECONOMY

The gig, creator, and consumer-to-consumer economies enable every one of us to build an audience and monetize our talents.

Most creations of the arts, music, marketing, and even technologies are not original. They are mostly made of existing ideas that are combined and transformed into something new.

Everyone can build an audience

For the longest time, creativity was the exclusive domain of a microscopic group of artists, designers, and advertising professionals. Today, we all create pictures and videos for social media, which we often stage and modify using filters and graphic effects. We visit museums online and offline, discover new artists through social media, and co-create products with brands such as Nike, DeWalt, and LEGO.

For those of us who want to be in front of the camera, it is now easier than ever to be discovered and monetize our audience. In the legacy entertainment industry, creators were discovered by an agent or studio, which then would cultivate their image over time. Today, talents can grow their audience quickly via platforms like YouTube, Instagram, TikTok, Medium, or Substack.

Such platforms are accessible to everyone and offer extensive tools to create, scale, and monetize content and audiences, greatly contributing to making the creator industry the fastest growing small business segment; more than 50 million people consider themselves creators or influencers.[1]

These platforms help make creativity more accessible and act as gate-keepers to mass audiences, not unlike the traditional record labels, movie studios, and TV producers.

In the creator economy, platforms productize knowledge or skills in new ways, thereby normalizing and broadening new paths to work. Further, they offer extensive functionalities tailored to e-commerce merchants, including a network of fulfillment centers, marketing and SEO solutions, and merchant cash advances, to name but a few services.

The creator economy is also transforming news and media organizations. Between 2008 and 2019, the United States lost half of its newsroom employees as local news coverage, in particular, collapsed. Not only are circulation numbers free-falling, but most of the advertising revenue is also being captured by Facebook and Google. Enter newsletter platforms like Substack, Facebook Bulletin, and Revue, which enable writers to charge their subscribers for their newsletter. Some argue that these newsletters are mostly made of commentaries and are cheaper and faster to produce than legit news, which requires extensive research, fact-checking, and editing.

As in the movie and music industries, traditional news and media organizations are no longer the gatekeepers of information. Some argue that news organizations have long betrayed the trust readers placed in them, often disregarding their own rules of independence, disclosure of compromise, vetting of the reporting, and editorial oversight.[2]

Whether it is in journalism, music, arts, or writing, everyone now has access to tools to build an audience. The challenge is no longer to access the audience but to stand out and amplify a message. Take music, for example; 90 percent of all streams on Spotify are shared between 43,000 artists, and 40,000 tracks are uploaded on Spotify every day. With the conservative assumption that Spotify hosts tracks for 3 million artists, that means 98.6 percent of artists (2,957,000) share 10 percent of the streams. Based on Spotify's notes to investors, 10 percent of Spotify's recorded music payments equals about $107 million. Divided among 2.6 million artists, that means each of them earns an average of $12/month.[3]

How Taylor Swift is taking control

In August 2019, Taylor Swift announced she would rerecord her pre-Republic Records discography as soon as she was legally allowed to. By doing this, Swift bypassed Shamrock Holdings, which owns the rights to her first six records.[4] Note that songs on her album *Red (Taylor's Version)* are nearly identical covers of her early recordings.

Swift asked her fans to play only the records she rerecorded and asked brand partners to use these in advertisements, TV shows, movies, and games.

Demonstrating the power of her fan following, the songs Taylor Swift rerecorded outperformed their original counterparts on streaming services and social media, leading to lucrative licensing deals.[5] For example, "Wildest Dreams (Taylor's Version)" has been used in over 70,000 TikTok videos and viewed over 2 billion times. In contrast, the original was used in fewer than 7,000 videos.

This illustrates the shifting power dynamics in the music industry, whereby closed-door meetings in Hollywood don't rule over fans and artists and their followings. Propelled by streaming and direct access to fans, Swift inspired other artists to rerecord their songs and control their music. When negotiating their contracts, many artists are now seeking ownership of their master recordings to assert more control over the way their music is used and the profits it generates. A label typically receives up to 80 percent of the streaming revenue; artists who control their master recordings enjoy 80 to 95 percent.

Looking forward

Talent will become more focused on specific vertical interests and passions. For example, in cooking, we'll see influencers attracting audiences around a specific type of recipe or cooking style. Viewers will select content based on their interests and the credentials and credibility of the creator, more so than on the name and personality of the content creator.

In the meantime, changes are underway in the advertising industry. Advertisers soon won't be able to track individuals online. Brands will have a harder time reaching their audience. Influencer marketing and content creation will become the most efficient way to reach consumer audiences. To succeed, brands must give up some creative control; what is most valuable to brands is the relationship between the talent and their audience through the content produced. Therefore, brands should refrain from imposing creative guidelines that would be too stringent.

A contemporary expression of creativity: Francis Bourgeois and Gucci

Luxury consumers are no longer solely focused on jewelry and handbags. People, especially men, now mix and match designer clothing with more functional garments that are fit for movement. That's why US department store Nordstrom adopted cross-merchandising, putting Nike next to Balenciaga and Valentino next to Vans. For the same reason, luxury Italian brand Gucci partnered with American outdoor brand The North Face to draw connections between luxury, adventure, and streetwear. To promote their collaborative line, the two brands rely on what their agency (Highsnobiety) describes as "eccentric exploration," a "luxuriously vintage, dreamlike lifestyle."[6] The agency created campaigns that allow playfulness and eccentricity, breaking down the clichés of what outdoor recreation is like. For the first installment of the campaign, Highsnobiety paired Gucci and The North Face with the birdwatching club "Flock Together."[7] Bird watching, fishing, foraging, and the Japanese tradition of forest bathing are gaining popularity and attracting a broad demographic that goes well beyond the stereotype of the gray-haired white male. This partnership conveys the values the brands advocate: nature does not discriminate and the outdoors are inclusive of different cultures and ethnic backgrounds. Just like wearing The North Face and Gucci, nature is a place where everyone can express themself creatively with no fear of judgment.

For its second campaign, Highsnobiety enlisted British train-spotting enthusiast Francis Bourgeois, who happens to draw 2.2 million fans on TikTok. Known for his eccentricity and self-embracing attitude, Bourgeois assumes the roles of both ticket inspector and conductor, leading his co-travelers (adorned with Gucci and The North Face gear) through an idealized train journey. Beyond a mere brand spokesperson or "influencer," Bourgeois is a true creator as he develops his unique, distinct creative style and informs fashion trends and cultural moments.

> The linearity in the predictability of trains satisfies the side of my brain that likes to know how things are done. Then the spontaneity and unpredictability of the nature of trainspotting itself fulfill the other side of my brain that goes "Oh what's going to happen next?"
>
> —FRANCIS BOURGEOIS, TRAIN SPOTTER

The gig economy

In contrast with the creator economy, which emphasizes the creativity and uniqueness of its contributors, the gig economy tends to commoditize its workers. For example, Uber limits interactions between customers and providers, whereas Substack and Medium encourage interactions between creators and customers.

That said, strong parallels are now emerging between the gig economy and the creator economy. Creators are progressively losing leverage to the marketplace gatekeepers that control the creators' audience and it is difficult to migrate one's audience to any other platforms. "Deplatforming" results in the loss of a creator's audience and past creations.

As with all e-commerce players, marketplaces for the gig and creator economies heavily invest in collecting and analyzing data, such as the skills and credentials of all network participants, their location, feedback scores, rates, all tasks they completed, and interactions with the network. This network effect exponentially strengthens the grip of these platforms over their members and the market overall; they own the data, social graphs, and relationships with end users. In this process, creators become a de facto unpaid workforce and, eager to get more visibility, post a large amount of content that they often produce for free. This content generates visitor traffic, which marketplaces subsequently monetize through advertising.

Sometimes called service reselling or service arbitrage, *drop servicing* is inspired by the drop-shipping model, where a retailer sells physical goods online that it neither produces nor even stocks. Instead, the retailer orders directly from the manufacturer, who ships the order to the buyer. Drop servicing applies the model, whereby a middleman resells the services of voice-over artists, copy writers, graphic designers, and other skilled freelance workers.

Drop servicers juggle clients and the freelancers they source on marketplaces such as Fiverr, marking their services up as much as 500 percent.[8] That is made possible by the intense competition between gig workers, who charge as little as $250 for the post-production of a wedding video, or a few dollars for a logo. Admittedly, this model has been in existence in the corporate world for years but servicing mostly outsourced labor to English-speaking workers in countries where labor costs cents on the dollar compared to Europe and North America.

There are even drop servicing influencers, who publish "get rich quick" videos where they promise huge returns for very little. Perhaps what is most concerning is to see these videos on TikTok, where these new snake oil salesmen are as young as 13. Aspiring drop servicers can purchase courses from such "mentors" for under $300, and supposedly learn how to find clients, brand their newly minted business, and earn hundreds of dollars with a few hours of work a week.

The consumer-to-consumer economy

Platforms such as Patreon and Twitter Blue connect customers and creators so that customers get involved in the artist's creative process. In return, they get access to exclusive content and benefits.

SPOTLIGHT ON | ETSY

At the beginning of the global pandemic in April 2020, Etsy made its mark selling facemasks, an item that was meaningful to users. Now, Etsy's sales have surged across a wide range of products, including gardening kits, beauty products, and self-care. Even baked goods sales have surged. This phenomenon benefits the 3.7 million "makers" or sellers who currently leverage the power of Etsy to build their business.[9]

Bolstered by a 119 percent growth in 2020, Etsy invested in ad campaigns that focused on human connection, diversity, acceptance, and togetherness. "The common thread is the power of personalized, unique items," says Etsy CMO Ryan Scott. In fact, "personalized gift" was the most-searched term on Etsy last year, Scott said. In a world where everything is disposable, fast, and cheap, Etsy fills that gap by providing goods worth keeping, such as a handmade mug we use ritually for our first cup of coffee in the morning. Brands and products that carry flaws convey authenticity and proximity. Products sold on Etsy contribute to a keener sense of self for consumers because these products reflect who we are and who we want to be.

Etsy recognizes the challenges makers/sellers often have to overcome to pursue their passions as creative business owners. In its advertising spot "Making of Makers," Etsy highlights the commonalities between makers and athletes; both succeed through their dedication to the craft, focus on skills and technical precision, and the pursuit of a lifelong passion.

Etsy's success is also fueled by our longing for when the future seemed less worrisome and our lives were simpler. To reconnect with the past, we recall joyful memories that turn negative feelings positive, boost our self-esteem, and enhance our mood. We do so through familiar brands and objects that transport us to another time by evoking the same feelings we experienced so long ago. Nostalgia also increases our feeling of social connectedness and gives us a more positive outlook on the future.

Everything is a remix

Conventional wisdom suggests that true creators come up with novel ideas in sparks of genius. Many people don't see themselves as artists or creators or doubt their creative abilities because they believe that artists constantly reinvent the wheel.

In reality, most movies, songs, paintings, products, and books are inspired and informed by the work of other creators. They are "remixes": their creators collect, combine, edit, and rearrange existing materials to produce something new. Creating something new from something old has never been easier—digital media enables us to source, curate, and remix ideas from all over the world in seconds. Ultimately, very few creations are truly seminal, and marketing is no exception. Does this matter?

When done ethically, a remix credits the work of other contributors (this book includes well over 200 references). Also, remixing enriches existing work. Finally, drawing from existing music, books, and movies prompts familiar, positive emotions and recontextualizes them for the audience.

Steve Jobs, seen by many as the greatest inventor and entrepreneur of our time, freely admitted to being "shameless about stealing great ideas."[10]

> **It comes down to trying to expose yourself**
> **to the best things that humans have done.**
> **And then try to bring these things into**
> **what you are doing […] we always**
> **have been shameless about stealing great ideas.**
>
> —STEVE JOBS[11]

Copy / transform / combine

George Lucas, Led Zeppelin, and Steve Jobs are geniuses that brought us *Star Wars,* "Stairway to Heaven," and the Apple Macintosh. Or did they? *Star Wars* was based on *The Hero with a Thousand Faces*, a book by Joseph

Campbell. The famous opening to "Stairway to Heaven" is heavily inspired by Spirit's 1968 "Taurus," and Apple's mouse came from Xerox.

I spoke with filmmaker Kirby Ferguson, who popularized the "copy/transform/combine" process. Ferguson argues that this is a consistent pattern and the formula for innovation. As such, the typewriter is modeled upon a piano; rock and roll is a transformation of the American blues.

Copy

Copying requires people to be curious, open to a wide range of influences, and select the ones that feel most promising and unfamiliar. To copy, you must gather disparate raw materials and revisit them several times to tease out a pattern or something intriguing you can expand upon.

Transform

Transforming involves creating variations of these raw materials and influences. Ferguson describes the process of transformation as gradual modifications. To transform, Ferguson experiments with associating disparate ideas and making creative leaps.

Combine

This last step of the process is about connecting and merging multiple ideas in a new and creative way. What is most compelling and yields the best results is the combination of ideas, products, or people that don't intuitively fit together. In advertising, examples of quirky combinations include Gucci using the vintage aesthetic of a train journey through the Alps, and BIC's ad featuring rapper Snoop Dogg and Martha Stewart.

> It's much easier to improve on somebody else's idea
> than it is to create something from scratch.
> To be original, you don't have to be the first, you just
> have to be different and better.
>
> —ADAM GRANT[12]

Be ready to be copied

So how does it feel to see other people borrowing your ideas? Put it this way: you are welcome to steal part or even all the ideas outlined in this book; I even encourage you to do so.

If you borrow an idea, it suggests that you find it valuable. Also, if you credit me for the idea, it will give more visibility to my work and my brand. Remixing drastically increases the reach of ideas that would have otherwise remained arcane.

For example, Seth Godin, one of the most sought-after marketing thought leaders of our times, published a book in 2008 called *Tribes: We Need You to Lead Us.*[13] *Tribes* show how people are keen on connecting around an idea with the guidance of a leader. Godin argues that the internet helps create and grow tribes, presenting opportunities for consumers, marketers, and investors, among others.

While compelling, neither the concept of tribes nor its marketing application is new. Tribes have existed for thousands of years in religious, political, economic, and ethnic contexts. In the field of marketing, academics like Bernard Cova had pointed to the importance of communities and consumption as early as 1997.[14] The idea of tribal consumption and tribal marketing are further described in academic articles published in 2001[15] and 2002.[16]

Seth Godin did not invent the concept of tribe nor its marketing application. His contribution was to build on an idea to make it relevant, approachable, and actionable for a much wider audience. Had it not been for Godin's book, Cova's ideas—originally titled "Community and consumption: Towards a definition of the linking value of products or services" and "Tribal aspects of postmodern consumption research: The case of French in-line roller skaters"—would likely have never gained traction outside of a few elitist academic circles.

> **If you want to be original, be ready to be copied.**
> —COCO CHANEL

Remixing prompts questions about intellectual property and plagiarism. And as we will see in the Pharrell Williams case covered in Chapter 10, remixing can lead to lengthy and expensive lawsuits, especially when the remixed version of an existing idea becomes more successful than the original.

How creators and brands should approach remixing

Let go of your impostor syndrome and insecurities

People will steal your ideas and that's fine, especially because you too steal from others. What's most important is you constantly seek new material so that you always work on three to five new ideas and stay ahead of everyone else.

Identify what you love to do and what you do well

Get specialized: You're not just interested in cooking; you are on a quest to find the best Neapolitan pizza. You're seeking to create the perfect ice cream, not take over the dairy market (yet).

Define and reach your audience

Too much emphasis has been put on the number of "friends" and "likes." Instead of aiming for quantity, identify your minimum viable market; your audience might seem small at first sight, but what matters is for people to engage with you and your brand, not just "follow" you.

Sell on value, not on price

As discussed in this chapter, online marketplaces such as Upwork and Fiverr connect talent with clients at scale. However, they facilitate a race to the bottom, a sort of reversed auction that cheapens skills and talent.

Keep in mind going market rates. Sell your work on value, not on price. There will always be a cheaper option anyway. Also, your client will take your rates for granted: it will be incredibly hard to raise your prices in the future, so resist the urge of discounting.

Sell the experience

Starbucks doesn't sell coffee; people couldn't tell Starbucks apart from competitors in a blind taste test. Starbucks is neither the home nor the office. It is a multi-sensory experience made of the smell of coffee, curated music, your interaction with a barista, and the enjoyment of a handcrafted beverage.

> Good artists copy; great artists steal.
> —T. S. ELIOT (1920S), OR PICASSO (1952), OR STEVE JOBS (1995)[17]

KEY TAKEAWAYS ✸ ✸ ✸

- Creativity is no longer the exclusive domain of a microscopic group of artists, designers, and advertising professionals. Today, technology and digital media have made all of us artists, creators, and collectors.

- Platforms like YouTube, Substack, and Spotify are accessible to everyone and offer extensive tools to create, scale, and monetize content and audiences.

- In the creator economy, these platforms productize knowledge or skills in new ways, normalizing and broadening novel paths to work.

- In contrast with the creator economy, which emphasizes the creativity and uniqueness of its contributors, the gig economy tends to commoditize its workers.

- In the consumer-to-consumer economy, platforms such as Patreon and Twitter Blue connect customers and creators so that customers get involved in the artist's creative process in return for access to exclusive content and benefits.

- Conventional wisdom suggests that true creators come up with novel ideas in sparks of genius; in reality, most movies, songs, paintings, products, and books are inspired and informed by the work of other creators. They are remixes; their creators collect, combine, edit, and rearrange existing materials to produce something new. As such, you are welcome to copy part or even all the ideas outlined in this book; I encourage you to do so.

PART
3

HOW
BRANDS
CAN
TRANSFORM
THE WORLD

CITIZENS AND BRANDS ARE ACTIVISTS

Brands and advertisers are no longer the dominating force. Everybody now has the power to create content and brands. We advocate these brands, talk back at them, or even cancel them.

The lines between advertisers and journalists are increasingly blurring, making these relationships incestuous.

Consumers are empowered to co-create brands with marketers through product development, content creation, and marketing.

In June 2020, TikTok users and fans of Korean pop music fielded more than one million ticket requests for then-president Trump's campaign rally as a prank. Based on these bookings, the Trump campaign had gone to media outlets predicting a massive success for the candidate's event. Only 6,200 people showed up. Media outlets extensively relayed pictures of Donald Trump talking before hundreds of empty rows of the 19,000 seats in Tulsa's BOK Center.[1]

Recently, citizen activists have also taken on big banks and financial institutions. In January 2021, dying video game retailer GameStop reached an all-time high of $350 on the stock market, up from $19 a few days prior. The surge was driven by millennials and Gen Z traders who organized their action via Reddit, the popular social news aggregator and discussion website.

In this process, several well-established hedge funds that had shorted the stock suffered losses to the point of almost going bankrupt.[2]

Just these two examples show that citizens—and, by extension, consumers—have become more outspoken and are willing to take action against personalities, organizations, or brands that don't align with their values. Thanks to social media, we can easily and cheaply advocate, challenge, or boycott pretty much anything and anyone.

The woke culture

Woke is a political term of African American origin that means being alert to racial prejudice and discrimination—being aware and concerned with issues of social justice and racial justice. The term has recently been amplified by the Black Lives Matter movement and has transcended to other communities to include Asians, LGBTQ+, and Hispanics. Woke culture sheds light on what life is like for multiple communities in our society, aiming to tackle societal issues and combat misconceptions.

On the flip side, some companies leverage the woke movement to "woke-wash" their brands to drive more sales and profits instead of creating any real change. An example is sportswear apparel brand Lacoste, which once swapped its trademark crocodile logo to feature endangered species instead. But the public soon pointed out that Lacoste was selling "gloves made from deer leather" and "cow leather handbags" through its website.[3]

There is no shortage of brands engaging in good causes through products that drive awareness for the cause and sales. This sometimes leaves the public wondering if their brand supports the cause or is solely seeking to generate profit.

- In 2019, UK grocery retailer Marks & Spencer created a sandwich that came in a rainbow-colored package, the "LGBT," a play on the traditional bacon, lettuce, and tomato, to which M&S added guacamole. To its credit, M&S launched its LGBT+ sandwich to celebrate Pride month and raise money for LGBT charities. If the brand made a £10,000 donation to charities, cynics could argue that M&S generates that much in revenue in 23 seconds (M&S's revenue for 2019 was close to £14 billion).[4] "I don't applaud it. It's the sort of idea that only comes from middle management meetings," commented someone on social media. Another response: "All the gays love rainbows. And vegetables! I know! Gay sandwich wrapper!"[5]

- Irish fast-fashion retailer Primark made a similar mistake when releasing a line of Pride-themed T-shirts that were manufactured in Turkey, ranked one of the worst countries in Europe for LGBTQ+ rights.[6]

- In the United States, Nike hired football player and civil rights activist Colin Kaepernick after he kneeled during the national anthem to protest racism. If the sports apparel brand has a long history of taking a stance on social causes and is known to be genuine in its engagements, it is worth mentioning that its Kaepernick initiative has earned Nike $6 billion,[7] with online sales growing 31 percent during the 2018 Labor Day weekend, right after the campaign launched.[8]

- British retailer ASOS has made efforts to support refugees by creating an exclusive lingerie line in partnership with Help Refugees, an NGO that receives all profits from the collection.

- Luxury brand Gucci supported a student-led march against gun violence, and Balenciaga is working with the World Food Program to combat hunger.

Some companies commit to good causes even further by becoming B-Corporations, a certification that attests the brand has considered the impact of its decision on the public, society, and the planet. B-Corps include outdoor outfitter Patagonia, ice cream brand Ben & Jerry's, and fashion and apparel brands Athleta, Allbirds, and Eileen Fisher, to name a few examples.

> **It's not who I am underneath,**
> **but what I do that defines me.**
> —BATMAN (*BATMAN BEGINS*, 2005)

Brands must facilitate self-expression

Self-expressive brands enable us to express our inner selves, "the way others see me."[9] People who want to express their "real me" are more engaged with brands online and are motivated to co-create brand value. They become brand advocates. Ultimately, they are willing to pay a premium and will develop a long-term relationship with the brand.

Before co-creating, consumers must first trust and engage with the brand. Brands such as Nike, Smirnoff, and Old Spice enable their audience to transform their sneakers, define what makes nightlife original, and remix their advertising campaigns.

People often carefully select what brands they follow to curate their virtual identity and present an idealized version of themselves. They might follow these brands online but never consume them offline. While immediate, their relationship with the brand is also short-lived.

How Gucci enables its customers to express their individuality

On a more positive note, brands can be a source or symbol that consumers transfer meaning to, like a mirror that reflects the identity of the individual.[10] When we bond with a brand, it helps define us and presents us as we want to appear, generating passionate feelings, a phenomenon marketers refer to as *brand passion*. Brand passion is particularly valuable to brands, as it drives trust, self-expression, and self-brand integration.

Gucci's challenge was to find the right balance between appealing to old-money consumers and the younger generation. Gucci focused its strategy on offering exclusive products through a culture of inclusivity.

To its customers, Gucci is a bold and unapologetic expression of individuality and self-expression. As such, Gucci enables its customers to disregard traditional rules imposed by society, such as gender identification, how to express oneself, or what to wear. The brand is transformative in that it enables its clients to be who they want to be, no matter how much they differ from "the norm." Gucci was the first to offer a gender-neutral collection, MX, and promises to question how binary gender relates to our bodies.

Most other luxury brands focus on selling an unrelatable dream or showcasing their craftsmanship, a key attribute of luxury that is relevant but not personal. In contrast, Gucci tells stories that position the consumer as the hero rather than the brand and its products.

The confidence to complete a challenge:
SPOTLIGHT ON | THE IKEA EFFECT

Instant cake mixes were first introduced in the 1950s to simplify the lives of American housewives by minimizing the tasks involved in baking. Today, the global cake mix market is more than $1.2 billion,[11] but cake mixes initially failed because they made it too easy; housewives felt their skills and labor were undervalued. Based on this, manufacturers changed the formula to require adding an egg, leading home cooks to believe their labor was crucial in the baking of a great cake.

Researchers coined this psychological phenomenon the IKEA effect[12]—named after the Swedish retailer whose furniture requires assembly. Doing a bit of legwork increases our belief in the value of the product we created, even though a professional would have delivered a better result. What's more, consumers are willing to pay more to build things themselves.

However, the task should be simple enough to complete. If people spend too much time and effort building their creations or fail to complete the task, their perception of the value of the item decreases.

Consumers foster tribes around brands

The concept of consumer tribes emerged from academic research in the late 2000s and subsequently became popular in marketing circles through books such as Seth Godin's *Tribes*. The concept signals a departure from individualistic consumption (where consumers make decisions on their own, for themselves) toward tribal marketing. This notion recognizes that we don't define our lives through the individual consumption of products, but through social relationships and communities these products facilitate. Subsequently, marketers started to focus on developing brand cultures, brand communities, and brand tribes, all hoping to mimic the success of brands such as Disney.

The great limitation of this approach is that the next generation does not want to be part of the tribes of their parents and grandparents. Tribes also are kind of the opposite of exclusivity: very effective in growing sales with fans, not so much at growing broader appeal for the brand.

How brand tribalism made the success and subsequent failure of Harley-Davidson

In the 1990s and 2000s, Harley-Davidson was the pinnacle of marketing, with case studies on the brand pervading academic textbooks, marketing books, and magazines. The company had built a cult-like brand, synonymous with strength and freedom to explore. While Harley's bike performance is deemed as average, it stands out from all other brands thanks to its "potato-potato" noise, low torque, and rugged aspect. Harley is the poster child of brand tribes through its HOG (Harley Owner Group), a community for Harley enthusiasts that gathers more than a million members worldwide. From a high of 260,000 units sold in 2006, Harley shipped only 180,000 in 2020.[13] And besides the pandemic and the economic climate, a lot of this decline can be attributed to the brand being completely out of sync with today's buyer: overwhelmingly white, male, and over 50.

In contrast, today's buyers prioritize ease of transportation and lighter bikes over Harley's heavy, impractical ones. Younger consumers are all about sustainability, diversity, inclusion, and brands that make a positive impact on society, which seem to contrast with what Harley stands for. The Harley-Davidson brand is aging out with bleak prospects for shifting its image among younger generations. The brand also lacks a cultural icon. In 1969, the movie *Easy Rider* became a 90-minute ad depicting two bikers riding from LA to New Orleans through open country and desert lands. Today, one would be hard-pressed to find anyone with a sizable following on social media endorsing the brand.

The Harley-Davidson brand's rise to fame and subsequent demise is a humbling reminder to marketers that brands must constantly evolve to stay relevant.

Consumers create advertising and marketing for brands . . .

Consumer-generated advertising is similar to advertising on consumer-generated media. Think of sponsored posts, paid posts, or sponsored reviews. User-generated content builds brand awareness among relevant audiences and communities.

Brands can reach out to their audience to invite people to collaborate in the development of their campaigns, also known as a "communal branding" effort, where consumers share their ideas and expressions of what the brand means to them. These contributions are then integrated into the campaign and shared with the brand's core audience, creating a bond between the brand, brand champions, and the core audience.

Brands can also engage their consumers in the development of a product or campaign, known as a "communal research" effort.

. . . While brands hire journalists to create PR and marketing content

Journalists and public relations professionals rely on each other as part of a communication ecosystem. Journalists draw from PR materials to find interesting stories, and PR professionals rely on journalists to get their messages out. True journalists would choose whether to pursue a story and seek out different sides of an issue rather than just publishing PR materials almost verbatim.

If historically journalists initially had the upper hand in this balancing act, PR has become increasingly dominant in light of job cuts in newsrooms. US newsroom employment has fallen 26 percent from 2008 to 2020, a loss of 30,000 jobs.[14] The bulk of this decline was driven by falling subscriptions and ad revenue; revenue from classifieds, once newspapers' cash cow, has virtually vanished. Many journalists have fled the traditional publishing industry for more stable and lucrative positions as PR executives/brand journalists at large corporations.

Meanwhile, traditional media rely on content produced by brands and their PR representatives. Further, cash-strapped newsrooms are turning to sponsored content and advertorials to compensate for shrinking revenue. PR firms sometimes rely on questionable practices to direct media attention that journalists wouldn't otherwise consider newsworthy. One of these practices is *astroturfing*, leveraging social media to create fake grassroots support for a specific organization or issue by buying likes, shares, and engagements to create fake interest for a specific product, person, brand, or organization. Overall, news outlets become less trustworthy because the information is driven by PR execs focused on their clients' goals rather than journalists focused on the public's interest.

How brands can become trusted sources

Consumers no longer expect brands to merely market their products, but to provide reliable and accurate information, take a stance on social issues, and make a positive contribution to society and the community. At the same time, people are increasingly concerned about the spread of fake news, which impacts their perception of media channels, social media platforms, and brands.

This phenomenon is exacerbated by the fact that fake news spreads about six times faster and is 70 percent more likely to be retweeted than the truth, according to a study from the Massachusetts Institute of Technology published in *Science*. How can brands maintain and even earn more trust from their customers in this complicated landscape? This question becomes complicated as consumers demand brands take more of a role not just in a "purpose-driven" way, but an evolved one that includes supporting roles for the consumers themselves and a host of social issues. The following are three things brands can do to become trusted sources of information.

Brands should not associate with fake news

To reach larger audiences, brands often associate themselves with the most popular stories, whether these are true or fake. Publishers that propagate fake news often take advantage of advertisers by placing mainstream ads next to misleading articles, because known brands make the content look more credible. Brands can't merely ban specific keywords but must carefully select the publishers they advertise with.

Brands must provide content to educate and inform the public

Except for a few niche categories such as luxury, brands can no longer expect consumers to just fantasize about owning their products. They must also inform and educate the public. For example, Whole Foods puts posters around its stores that explain how to choose sustainable seafood. Its sustainability ranking has been created through a science-based, peer-reviewed approach done in partnership with the Blue Ocean Institute and Monterey Bay Aquarium.

Brands can inform and help tackle social issues

When appropriate, brands can speak out about social issues, although they should focus on contributing to change rather than making a vague, washed-out statement. For example, Ben & Jerry's has a long history of championing social causes such as marriage equality and climate activism. Most recently, the ice cream brand teamed up with Vox Media and the Who We Are project to create a podcast that will look at segregation and the violence Black people face in America.

The post-purpose role of brands

People expect brands to play new roles

Brands can no longer merely advertise their products; they must also educate consumers in their area of expertise. In a recent Ipsos study on brand truth, 7 in 10 people said they hold tech companies responsible for educating people on using their software and platforms. That's why Microsoft plans to provide digital skills training for 25 million people this year under a new multi-million-dollar initiative. The initiative will bring together multiple branches of the company, including LinkedIn and GitHub. In a similar vein, Google offers free training, tools, and resources to help people grow their digital skills, career, and business. In particular, Grow with Google can teach business owners how to manage their business remotely, create a website, and connect directly with their customers. In finance, people feel that financial services companies are responsible for educating people on topics like investment (74 percent), money management (73 percent), and saving (72 percent). Bank of America has a Better Money Habits initiative that provides free tools and practical training about money to help people make smarter financial decisions. In healthcare, respondents feel that healthcare companies are responsible for educating people on topics like diseases and symptoms (84 percent), physical fitness (82 percent), and leading a healthy lifestyle (80 percent).

Actions speak loudly

Brands must demonstrate their positive impact on society, not just talk about it. Ipsos's survey on brand truth reveals that participants expect tech platforms to actively enforce their standards of behavior (71 percent) and censor content proven to be misleading (68 percent). Further, people expect tech companies to support small businesses through economic recovery. And the younger people are, the more emphasis they place on tech brands' contributions (18–34: 62 percent; 35–54: 55 percent; 55+: 48 percent). During the pandemic, Salesforce, PayPal, and Slack teamed up with GoDaddy and 27 other companies to create "Open We Stand," a platform to help small businesses stay afloat amid the virus. American Express established "Stand for Small," a coalition of more than 40 companies across media, technology, consumer goods, professional services, and many other industries that provide meaningful support to small businesses as they navigate the effects of the pandemic.

Although the public's expectations had started shifting before COVID-19, the pandemic rushed brands to no longer *talk about* but *demonstrate* their positive impact on society; 60 percent of Americans (70 percent of Gen Z) are more likely to consider a brand if its stance on such issues as equality aligns with their own.

Education, economic recovery, and sustainability are just three of the initiatives the public seeks. But brands can also contribute to society through innovation, safeguarding users' data privacy, or protecting users from harmful online content, among other avenues. In any case, a brand's contribution must feel tangible and relatable. To do so, brands must move away from bold, vague mission statements and focus instead on *what your brand can do for me, my family, my business, and my community.*

Brand activism: Carrefour's black supermarket

Europeans have access to only 3 percent of the fruits and vegetables produced because of a law that deems the 97 percent of varieties that are not registered in the Official Catalogue of Authorized Species as illegal.

France's supermarket chain Carrefour decided to defy this law by creating "the black supermarket," where it sells "illegal" fruits and vegetables in defense of biodiversity. These supermarkets staged 600 forbidden varieties of fruits and vegetables in large herbariums, complete with posters of producers who had been sued by agrochemical lobbies. Visitors were encouraged to sign a petition to change the law, garnering over 85,000 signatures. Carrefour further broke the law by entering a five-year contract with illegal producers and even invited opinion leaders to a signature ceremony.

The campaign boosted store traffic by 15 percent and drove a 10 percent sales increase for its produce section. As a result of the extensive publicity the campaign received, the European Parliament reauthorized the cultivation and sale of farmers' seeds.

The advertising campaigns featured relatable outlaw producers holding a fruit or vegetable of their production, along with provocative taglines such as "Taste this forbidden pumpkin and you'll find the law disgusting" and "Ironically, these brussels sprouts are forbidden by Brussel's law."[15]

How brands can take a stand

Be mindful when aligning your brand with a cause. Today's discerning consumer can easily spot the difference between genuine purpose and marketing gimmicks. Consumers expect brands to not only claim but demonstrate their purpose; they will closely examine if the brand's operations align with its claimed values. Based on this, consumers will patronize, advocate, or possibly cancel brands.

The network effect

The network effect refers to a situation where the value of the product or service depends on the number of users, buyers, or sellers who leverage it. The greater the number of participants, the greater the value of the offering.

Benetton, the inventor of brand purpose

Luciano Benetton, founder of the eponymous group, and his then–art director and photographer, Oliviero Toscani,* are, in my view, the inventors of purpose-driven advertising. In the 1980s, the clothing brand started a series of provocative advertising campaigns that relied on shocking photographs to grab viewers' attention. These campaigns dealt with social and political issues such as AIDS awareness, child labor, poverty, war, pollution, and racial integration. Some of its most memorable ads featured a set of identical hearts with "white," "black," and "yellow" written on them, a gay interracial family, or a nun kissing a priest. Benetton and Toscani believed the point of Benetton's advertising was not to sell pullovers but to promote its image by drawing public attention to important societal themes. Luciano Benetton explained why he focused his advertisements on causes rather than products. "By removing these images from their familiar contexts and putting them in a new context, they are more likely to be noticed and given the attention they deserve as the viewer becomes involved in the process of answering the questions: What does this image mean? Why does this image appear with a Benetton logo? How do I feel about the subject of the image? What can I do?"[16]

*Toscani is as controversial as he is creative. After many widely publicized campaigns, he was forced out of the company in 2000 after a campaign featuring death row inmates generated extensive backlash from murder victims.[17] He returned in 2017 and exited again in 2020 over comments he made about the collapse of the Morandi Bridge in Genoa, Italy, where 43 people died.[18]

KEY TAKEAWAYS

- Citizens, and by extension consumers, have become more outspoken and are willing to take action against personalities, organizations, or brands that don't align with their values. Thanks to social media, we can easily and cheaply advocate, challenge, or boycott pretty much anything and anyone.

- Being *woke* means being aware and concerned with issues of social and racial justice and combating misconceptions.

- Self-expressive brands enable us to express our inner self—"who I truly am inside"—or enhance our social self. People who want to express their "real me" are more engaged with brands online and are motivated to co-create brand value.

- We carefully select what brands we follow on social media to curate their virtual identity and present an idealized version of ourselves.

- In sharp contrast with other luxury brands, Gucci enables its customers to disregard the traditional rules imposed by the society we live in, such as gender identification, how to express oneself, or what to wear.

- Doing a bit of legwork increases our belief in the value of the product we created, even though a professional would have delivered a better result. We overvalue what we created ourselves, even if it is adding an egg to a powder mix or assembling a standardized desk.

- Brands should be discriminating in their approach to brand safety—they can't merely ban specific keywords but must carefully select the publishers they advertise with instead.

- Brands must demonstrate their positive impact on society, not just talk about it.

THE NEW ERA OF BRAND RELEVANCE

When choosing a product, we do not think of brands and categories in isolation; we make our choice in light of the occasion and the particular needs associated with it.

Brands become more relevant by developing interconnected sets of products and services centered around the attitudes and aspirations of their target audience.

We have been on a treadmill to consume more for two centuries

The consumer society became a mass phenomenon in eighteenth-century Western Europe and we keep consuming more and more, tapping into seemingly infinite brands, products, and resources.

The Industrial Revolution led to many people leaving the agricultural countryside to work in larger cities, where they sought new ways of defining themselves, often through consumer goods. At the same time, shopkeepers experimented with merchandising, creating attractive window displays, and advertising in newspapers. In the United States, the consumerism movement accelerated in the 1920s, when instead of advocating a shorter workweek, people preferred to work full-time, even overtime, to earn and spend more.

Next came department stores, invented in the mid-nineteenth century in England, and then shopping malls in the United States in the early twentieth century. By the 1990s, oversized shopping malls, such as the Mall of America in Bloomington, Minnesota, opened to offer a plethora of stores along with entertainment options such as aquariums and an indoor roller coaster.

Consumerism has reached a new high since the 2000s, as the internet and social media give us access to copious advertising, celebrities, trends, products, and ways to flaunt our wealth.

The treadmill seems to keep accelerating, but who is increasing the speed?

- Marketers own their fair share of responsibilities in creating envy and desires for products we most often don't need.

- We compare ourselves to our friends, neighbors, and relatives and try to keep up with them.

- We also try to emulate the lives of celebrities, which is out of reach for most of us. One of the most successful reality television series of all time was *Keeping Up with the Kardashians*. The series, which ran for 20 seasons, depicted the life of a family that was famous for being famous and indulged in seemingly endless luxurious consumption. Owning the same handbag or drinking the same champagne as the Kardashians helped some live vicariously through them.

Running on this treadmill is starting to feel exhausting, and many of us are looking for a break.

Small is the new big

For 50 years, big media, big retailers, and big brands have ruled the world by focusing on scale to reduce costs from sourcing through manufacturing to marketing and overheads. Big brands would often reinvest these savings in innovation, giving them an advantage over the smaller players. The imperative of scale also created barriers to entry for the smaller players. Times have changed. From 2016 to 2020, extra-small manufacturers (with less than $100 million in sales), small manufacturers ($100 million to $999 million in sales), and private-label brands all gained market share at the expense of large manufacturers (more than $6 billion in sales).[1]

Today, small brands benefit from easier market access at small volumes. Unlike the traditional wholesale/large retail models, merchant tools and platforms like Shopify scale down to the needs and constraints of small merchants.

Small companies no longer need to invest in their own means of production. In buying or leasing excess production capacity from other brands, they can focus on innovation, marketing, and sales instead.

Small brands used to be hindered by few retailers carrying a limited number of brands along with their private labels. E-commerce has solved this by giving anyone access to an audience; Amazon shelf space is unlimited. From a marketing standpoint, social media and digital advertising enable small brands to target audiences without the large up-front commitments that traditional media command.

Bookshop.org: A socially conscious alternative to Amazon

Bookshop.org offers a socially conscious alternative to online shopping, offering its customers an Amazon-level of convenience while enabling them to support the local community. When launched in the UK in November 2020, Bookshop.org sold £65,000 worth of books without spending on any conventional media placement. Business peaked in June 2021 with sales of £1 million in a day.[2]

On Bookshop.org, customers search directly from the inventory of their local bookstore, which receives the profit from the order, or order without selecting a specific bookstore, in which case the profit goes into a pool redistributed among all participating bookstores across the country.

Do "ethical consumers" kid themselves?

Clients of Bookshop.org are arguably the ones most likely to shop from bookstores in the first place. By shopping on Bookshop.org, they might be buying a book they'd have bought from the store, further eating into the retailer's profit margin.

The future of retail

In numerous categories where physical product demonstration and trial are not important, physical stores will become a fulfillment channel more than a purchase channel. Stores are already increasingly becoming pick-up points and de facto fulfillment centers. Ultimately, brick-and-mortar stores will either focus on price, efficiency, and convenience or become venues for unique, premium experiences. These stores will deliver an immersive, multi-sensory experience that will combine technology and advice from highly-trained store assistants.

In Milan, Italy, Venetian fashion brand Slowear recently opened Slowear18, a space that hosts a fashion store, café, and a mixology bar. The versatile store furnishings serves as a product exhibit during the day and transforms into a display case and bar counter in the evening. Transparent cases enable cocktail bar patrons to see the clothes, and presumably come back during the day to try and buy them.[3]

Pop-up stores will also become increasingly prevalent. These stores bank on the novelty effect of a new collection or line of products and bypass the downsides of traditional retail such as long store leases, off-peak, unprofitable hours, and all-too-common staffing issues. Pop-up stores do not have to be based at traditional retail locations but can be set up in parks, town squares, parking lots, and even gardens.

SPOTLIGHT ON | FARROW & BALL

Farrow & Ball is a small manufacturer of paints and wallpapers from Dorset, England. But it does not just sell paint; it sells a lifestyle. Farrow & Ball is the paint of choice for New York's MoMA and Windsor Castle, among other prestigious residencies. It was one of the first companies in the UK to market paint as an aspirational product by connecting it to Britain's cultural and architectural heritage.

I had a chance to meet with Anthony Davey, CEO of Farrow & Ball, who shed light on the strengths and uniqueness of the company. The interview has been edited for clarity.

Emmanuel Probst: After spending 20 years at Procter & Gamble, arguably the largest consumer brand powerhouse in the world, what are the key learnings you brought to Farrow & Ball?

Davey: Founder/owner businesses in general (like Farrow & Ball) are built on somebody's great idea, which is often a new way to work in the category—and change the category. The founder can take the brand to a good place based on this disruptive idea, but only so far. Eventually, the founder/owners reach their limit, and the incumbent management says, What do we do now?

Founder/owner businesses like Farrow & Ball don't have all the processes of a P&G. They have a great idea, but the likes of P&G are pioneers in consumer understanding, consumer research, and product development.

For example, P&G really pioneered consumer research in neuroscience and synaptic readings. There is a lot of knowledge the big companies can bring to help the small companies move forward. With F&B, consumers fell in love with the brand, the concept, the experience, and then eventually, it went flat: we were only selling to our fans and charging a bit more, but we had to go find the right balance of new users and existing users. We couldn't have grown much more among our core audience. So we did some work to uncover what the brand stands for.

Probst: What about the retail experience?

Davey: First, all store associates have experience in design, expertise, knowledge, enabling the brand to deliver a very human, personalized consultation in-store. We also invest significantly in online business, next-day delivery, live chat . . . so if you want purely transactional, you can do that online. But if you want a consultation, you go in-store. We go further with consultation in your home with a color consultant: the consultant asks about the sun and where it rises. When, for example, the consultant identifies a given window that gets the sun in the evening, he will recommend a color that will be more pleasing based on the light and time of day. The color consultant service doesn't generate much profit, if any. The point of the service is to give people the confidence to create.

Probst: In terms of production capabilities, how does Farrow & Ball differ from the bigger brands?

Davey: You can't make our paint at high-speed, mass production levels. At P&G, we implemented the "RFT" process, which stands for Right First Time. When you mix toothpaste, for example, the blend needs to be 99.6 to 99.7 percent correct the first time so that the overall production can run more efficiently.

At Farrow & Ball, the Right First Time is only 60 percent: the other 40 percent is not good enough to meet our high standards for consistency of the colors. Although the mix is not wasted: we paint it, scan it, and measure the accuracy of all the batches. With the batches that don't meet our standards, we remix them with pigments and get it right the second time.

We can do this because we produce only 120 million pints. You cannot do this when you produce billions of liters of paint as the process cannot be interrupted.

Premiumization: Consume less but better

Premiumization is the process of motivating consumers to pay more for brands, products, and services and relies on raising a consumer's perceived value; if the item meets what the consumer wants and needs, they gauge if they are paying the right price for it.

For brands, premiumization is a way to diversify and innovate. For consumers, buying premium products is a way to reward themselves and can even be an act of self-care, which can justify a higher price point. This became even more important during the pandemic as people began to consider "me time" essential to well-being. Premium products must be justified by their benefits, ingredients, and processing. Examples include single-sourced chocolate and handcrafted goods.

Counterintuitively, the premiumization trend is supported by the growth of private-label brands such as Walmart's "Great Value" and Amazon's "Basics." Indeed, consumers seek these brands for everyday items that are "good enough" but don't justify spending more on a big brand name. This is particularly true of categories where distinctions between private label and name brands are barely perceptible. Anyone would be hard-pressed to articulate the difference between Clorox bleach and Target's Up

& Up, or Quilted Northern toilet paper and Presto!, its cheaper Amazon alternative. This helps explain why, in 2021, US private-label brands generated over $143 billion in sales, up from only $14 billion in 2015.[4]

The case for premium gin

This reasoning is particularly relevant in the alcohol category. For the last 20 years, consumers of wine and spirits have been drinking fewer, but more premium, beverages.

As people drink less, they want their choice of alcohol to reflect how special they are. Gin, for example, was not considered premium, while Bombay Sapphire, Gordon's, and Beefeater were all selling at fairly similar price points.

In 2015, Bombay Sapphire became increasingly aware of this lack of differentiation. It turned to the example of premium vodkas such as Grey Goose and Belvedere and created a gin with better flavors and a stylish, artfully designed bottle. Bombay Sapphire marketed this product as a high-end gin selling for almost €20 when mainstream gins like Tanqueray sell for about half that. Its premium gin drove the category upmarket and contributed to making gin hip and popular.

Eventually, its €20 gin became mainstream, prompting Bombay Sapphire to sell higher-end gins, in the €30 to €50 range. In the meantime, smaller companies started developing even more expensive "boutique gins" infused with botanicals and cocoa. Most recently, Instagram made the color pink popular, particularly among young females. In response to this trend, manufacturers started making "Instagram-worthy" pink gins. Today, pink gins account for 14 percent of the market across 150 different gins.[5]

Contextual commerce: May I have your attention, please?

Contextual commerce is about enabling people to buy something as soon as they discover it. Amazon Prime members expect their purchases to be delivered the next day or even the same day. Uber has trained us to get a ride within a few minutes, and Netflix allows us to watch one of its 3,700-plus movies in seconds.[6]

With contextual commerce, people can buy anything at any time without interrupting their lives. They do so at the click of a button, voice response, or through their AI-powered device. The point of contextual commerce is to reduce the time lag between discovery and purchase while doing something else, such as cooking or commuting. Contextual commerce relies on technologies such as automatic speech recognition and natural language processing to allow computers to convert speech into text and orders.

Visual search is among the most promising technologies that power contextual commerce. eBay, Google, Amazon, and Pinterest let users upload photos they have taken to search for items featured in the pictures. In retail, IKEA and Argos offer shoppers augmented reality features that enable them to visualize items in their homes without having to measure or wrestle to match colors and styles.

How brands can harness contextual commerce

While contextual commerce presents opportunities for brands to shorten their consumers' journey, the technology it relies on will further exacerbate the dominance of fewer brands. For example, a search on Amazon for "AA batteries" returns more than 10,000 results. Statistically, over 90 percent of shoppers pick a brand from the first page; the following pages make up less than 9 percent of clicks.[7] Shoppers, therefore, choose from 33 results across eight brands: "Amazon Basics" (which turns out to be "Amazon's Choice"), Duracell, Energizer, Rayovac, ACDelco, LiCB, or Kodak.

> **The best place to hide a dead body**
> **is page two of Google.**
>
> —CHAD POLLITT, CONTRIBUTOR, *HUFFPOST*[8]

Running the same search via voice with Amazon Alexa will return only two results: Amazon Basics and Duracell. Realistically, no one would listen to 33 search results from Alexa, let alone memorize and compare price points across that many options. Ultimately, consumers will end up choosing from fewer brands and potentially buying the same product at a higher price point.

Contextual commerce is particularly suited for monetizing brands' content strategy, whereby brands can seed products throughout the educational content they disseminate rather than just advertising. An efficient content strategy also helps reduce returns as consumers access more information about the product to ensure they select the best option to fulfill their needs.

Contextual commerce helps brands significantly raise awareness and relevance as consumers see how the product or service can benefit them in the context of their everyday lives. Further, it facilitates higher conversions as today's shoppers are overwhelmed with digital ads and get easily frustrated with friction-filled buying experiences.

Last but not least, data analytics and artificial intelligence allow companies to analyze people's past purchases, then predict future purchases and offer suggestions and recommendations for products that are most relevant to each shopper.

Starbucks, for example, leverages contextual commerce to personalized offers in real time. It analyzes data collected in-store and through its loyalty program to serve updates and personalized offers via its app and emails.

The ecosystem-driven growth

Brands have become smarter about expanding their reach through a set of coherent products and services. Some become lifestyle brands centered around the attitudes and aspirations of their target audience. The most successful ones become ecosystems: an interconnected set of services that enables users to fulfill a wide range of needs in one integrated experience.

Ecosystem brands serve as one-stop shops for all consumer needs. These brands derive real benefits from the network of connections and interactions they can create with their customers, provided that data is collected, integrated, and leveraged smartly.

Google, Apple, and Amazon are "master" ecosystem brands; their platforms allow multiple merchants and consumers to interact with each other and create and exchange value. Not all brands can realistically cover such extended relationships with their customers, but there is room for smaller, highly specialized ecosystem brands, particularly for products and services that stay offline by nature.

Silicon Valley's holy grail is product-market fit. But today's winners, realizing that there are so many products and limited markets, think about what they're bringing to the world differently. For them, it's about solution-need fit, where knowing your customers and their current needs, anticipating their future needs, and exceeding their expectations around fulfilling needs at any point in time results in solutions that serve, rather than products to push. With an acute awareness of and fastidious focus on needs, success comes from effectively solving for the opportunity and reducing friction points—*beyond* whatever your immediate product offers. Through a combination of sensitivity, speed, and agility, innovation stems from the world of opportunity—the ecosystem—around a need. This evolved offer is much more than a brand extension (which often tackles the same need differently); instead, it addresses peripheral needs surrounding the core one, creating more numerous and more powerful synapses that not only forge stronger connections with more satisfied customers but equip brands with critical insight and ammunition to continue feeding the flywheel. Among the numerous competitive advantages that brands exhibit, it is worth noting the following.

Ecosystem brands excel at delivering customer intimacy and personalization

More knowledge of customers (especially on a per-customer basis) means greater familiarity with key audiences at each stage of the funnel. Ecosystem brands collect a plethora of data across services at the user level.

They can then model this data to personalize the customer experience and subsequently anticipate the user's needs, optimize the timeliness and effectiveness of their marketing, upsell companion products, and convert deflectors. Winning brands further leverage this multifaceted view of their customers to constantly refine the personalization of the experience, better anticipate future trends, and inform their product innovation efforts.

Ecosystem brands foster long-term loyalty

Ecosystems appeal to the head, heart, and hands to create solutions for real wants and needs; they craft experiences that not only live up to standards set by other categories and companies but also seamlessly integrate into lives and become objects of desire. Ecosystem brands also develop system-wide loyalty programs that are more rewarding for members and enable the ecosystem to easily unify the data it collects. For example, the Virgin Red loyalty program personalizes its member experience based on data gathered from the media you consume (Virgin Media), your workout (Virgin Active), the trains you ride (Virgin Train), and how you bank (Virgin Money).

Ecosystem brands enjoy a greater return on ad spend than any other brands

In an ecosystem, the advertising deployed to promote one service indirectly benefits all the others. When Microsoft advertises its Surface product, the campaign also drives awareness of its Office 360 brand and equity for its Microsoft master brand. Ecosystem brands can measure and optimize the impact of each campaign on each product, brand, and master brand. They can also measure the cumulative effect of different campaigns and optimize the sequencing of these campaigns and their components (media channels, publishers, creatives . . .) to maximize return on ad spend.

With all the options available, the winning formula is less about what brands offer and more about customer centricity (the human) and market responsiveness (their reality). As such, ecosystem-driven growth is the new era of brand building.

The most effective ecosystems are defined not by costs and defending of market share but by revenues and the creation of *new* markets altogether that better satisfy real needs. Realizing that expectation is reality, instead of a cheap price, these players battle for better—better quality, convenience, speed, and relevance.

DTC, for example, is not a channel: it's a personally and emotionally rewarding interaction with your local bakery instead of a cold, mission-accomplished, unfulfilling mass-produced dessert from the nearest grocer. The dialogue between the brand and the consumer is, therefore, more authentic, because it's rooted in delivering real value to the human rather than merely chasing a share of his wallet.

The occasion-driven growth

Pernod Ricard, the world's second-largest wine and spirits seller, centers its brand and communication efforts on consumers' Moments of Consumption, also called "Moments of Convivialité." During these moments, consumers do not think of brands and categories in isolation as they choose a drink. Rather, they make their choice in light of the occasion itself and the particular needs associated with it.

Absolut Vodka, for example, does not just compete with other vodka brands. When hosting an informal get-together with friends, a consumer might also drink a glass of whiskey and a glass of white wine. During a big night out, this same consumer might consider alternatives, such as a gin and tonic or a glass of champagne. To uncover insights from these Moments of Convivialité, Pernod Ricard and Ipsos developed a measurement program that integrates large volumes of unstructured data sourced from survey-based quantitative research and social media listening. To process and analyze this data in near real time, Ipsos relies on decision intelligence, a discipline that complements data science with social science theory, decision theory, and management science.

To deliver on this goal, the measurement program identifies key attributes to generate meaningful connections with consumers across each product in the portfolio.

With this bottom-up approach, the outputs are reviewed and interpreted by researchers, who provide cultural context, category expertise, and uncover unexpected insights. Pernod Ricard's bottom-up approach is now fueled by three years of back data, alongside real-time data, to track the size, brand fit, evolution of Moments of Convivialité, and new consumer behavior.

Ipsos applies topic modeling analysis, whereby large volumes of qualitative data are structured into topics that reflect consumers' spontaneous expressions about champagne and spirit brands. This analysis reveals the image saliency of Pernod Ricard's brands among their competitive sets. The topics modeled, such as *"A drink for casual gatherings"* and *"My favorite strong drink,"* then serve as common dimensions for all tracked brands.

Beyond topic modeling, social listening enabled by AI permits PRIME to quantify large volumes of social media mentions, which are organized into specific rational and emotional attributes such as *"High-quality product"* and *"A drink for lovers."* This AI or decisional intelligence tool provides a relevant approach for real-time and retrospective analysis of the incremental or disruptive evolution of the brand and its market. For example, during and after the lockdown, social media data combined with Quant Data and AI algorithms were able to detect, track, understand, assess, and value the changing mindset of consumers, ranging from the astonishment and disillusionment at the creation of new expertise (for example, mixology at home) and practices (new ways of meeting) to experience new and changed moments and live them fully.

The versatility of the framework also allows the analyst to deal with more traditional areas such as campaign impact and insight analytics where social data is analyzed to quantify performance and shed light on phenomena, which are then developed as hypotheses that the survey data analysis test confirms or denies (e.g., the impact on the imagery of interest to the brand), following well-established marketing science statistical inference methodologies.

This measurement program also enables point-in-time context analysis, such as understanding the impact of COVID-19 and the associated lockdowns on consumer attitudes and behavior. Finally, it measures the effect of commercial and marketing activities, which informs both its short-term and long-term brand strategies.

KEY TAKEAWAYS

- Since consumer society became a mass phenomenon in eighteenth-century Western Europe, we keep consuming more and more, tapping into seemingly infinite brands, products, and resources.
- For 50 years, big media, big retailers, and big brands have ruled the world by focusing on scale to reduce costs from sourcing through manufacturing to marketing and overheads.
- Today, small brands benefit from easier market access at lower volumes.
- In numerous categories where physical product demonstration and trial are not important, physical stores will become a fulfillment channel more than a purchase channel. Pop-up stores will also become more prevalent.
- Premiumization is the process of motivating consumers to pay more for brands, products, and services and relies on raising a consumer's perceived value of it.
- Counterintuitively, the premiumization trend is supported by the growth of private-label brands such as Walmart's "Great Value" and Amazon's "Basics." Consumers seek these brands for everyday items that are "good enough."

- Contextual commerce enables people to buy something as soon as they discover it.

- Contextual commerce is particularly suited for monetizing brands' content strategy, whereby brands can seed products throughout the educational content they disseminate rather than just advertising these products.

- Brands have become smarter about expanding their reach through a set of coherent products and services. The most successful ones become ecosystems: an interconnected set of services that enables users to fulfill a wide range of needs in one integrated experience.

- Brands can also grow by focusing on the occasion that drives consumers to buy a specific product. To identify these occasions, brands must implement measurement tools that capture consumers' attitudes in their own words and pictures.

THE IMPERATIVE FOR RESPONSIBLE CONSUMERISM

After years of over-consumption, we aim to buy more responsibly, keep products longer, and give these products a second life once we dispose of them.

Brands must implement responsible business practices that are considerate of the environment and encourage repairing, recycling, and reselling their products.

As consumers, we are drowning in stuff, tears, and trash

Consumer spending in the United States hit an all-time high of $13.3 trillion in the third quarter of 2019, up from $10.5 trillion in 2010 and $8.2 trillion in 2000.[1] We are spending more than ever on personal care items, consumer electronics, and clothes. The average American buys 66 garments a year.[2]

Consuming has become easier, as we no longer have to comply with restrictive store hours. Goods have become cheaper, even when we must ship them halfway around the globe. We also dispose of the products we buy faster than ever when they reach programmed obsolescence or simply because we get bored with them.

Most of these products end up in landfills; the average American disposes of 4.4 pounds of trash every day, which translates into 728,000 tons of daily garbage, or 63,000 garbage trucks full.[3] Every year, we throw away 9 million tons of furniture, 9.4 million tons of consumer electronics,[4] and 14 million tons of clothing (double the 7 million tons tossed 20 years ago).[5]

The more we consume, the lonelier we feel

We consume all these goods because marketing convinced us they can make us happy, loved, and esteemed. Consumerism works its way into our psyches and encourages us to structure our life around owning more goods. However, research shows that the more people value materialism, the lower their happiness and life satisfaction and they experience fewer pleasant emotions. Indeed, people who value the promises encouraged by consumer society are more likely to experience anxiety, substance abuse, and depression.

People who are bombarded with messages that urge them to acquire more stuff show decreased well-being and social disengagement.[6] Younger generations are the most affected; almost half of millennials and Generation Z report feeling lonely and isolated.[7]

That said, the problem might not be consumerism per se, but rather the brands and products themselves. If we trash the clothes, furniture, and electronics we bought recently, it is because we don't feel emotionally connected to the object or the brand. We are overwhelmed with the hundreds of brands and thousands of products to choose from. For example, there are over 190 brands of bottled mineral water in the United States, nearly quadruple the number available in 1998. Yet, blind tests show that consumers don't recognize any of the named brands, sometimes even preferring tap water over a bottle of $2.49 Fiji Natural Artesian Water.[8]

It is time to pivot toward more meaningful and responsible consumption choices. It is time to favor goods and services that are more eco-conscious and sustainable.

Who should be responsible for combating the climate crisis?

Ipsos Global Trends 2021 shows that 83 percent of people believe we are heading for an environmental disaster unless we change our habits quickly,[9] yet only 31 percent believe their country has a clear plan in place for how people, government, and businesses are going to unify to tackle climate change.

People feel the burden of responsibility. In a global survey from Ipsos,[10] 72 percent agreed that if ordinary people do not act now to combat climate change, they will be failing future generations, and 68 percent said that if companies do not act to combat climate change, they are failing their employees and customers. Globally, 65 percent believe that if their government does not combat climate change, it is failing citizens. Governments design policies that strive to combat the global climate crisis which companies must adhere to. Consumers also prompt brands to become more sustainable. When asked, "Who should be responsible for finding a way to reduce unnecessary packaging?," 40 percent of people surveyed said everyone, 38 percent said manufacturers and retailers, and only 3 percent said consumers alone. Product packaging is something that brands (not consumers) own and control, yet consumers influence business decisions by which brand they buy, based on its environmental impact.

Further, brands must confront pressure groups. One example is Badvertising, whose recent campaign to call out advertising agencies accused them of "greenwashing" consumers on behalf of their brand clients with high carbon footprints, willingly misleading consumers to believe that the advertised products are more environmentally friendly than they are, using words like "ethical," "conscious," or "sustainable" in their messaging. When it comes to implementing sustainable practices, organizations face a monumental task as they rarely control their entire supply chain ecosystem. London's Heathrow Airport, for example, recently committed to becoming carbon neutral by 2030, but only for the parts of the airports it runs. It excluded the emissions of the 1,300 flights that take off or land there every day.

What we believe contrasts with how we shop

While people claim to be concerned with the environment, their efforts to live in a more environmentally friendly way often fall short, and they default on easier actions. An Ipsos study revealed that almost 90 percent worldwide are confident in recycling and using low-energy lightbulbs. Conversely, only 55 percent would consider switching to a mostly plant-based diet, and 59 percent would avoid driving a car and long-distance air travel. When it comes to shopping, Ipsos Essentials data shows that globally, just over half of citizens consider themselves to be ethical or sustainable shoppers. In the United States, only 24 percent of shoppers see sustainability as a crucial factor when making a purchase, compared to 53 percent who say the same for affordability and 71 percent for quality. In baby and toddler products, for example, an Ipsos study showed that sustainability was not a top priority. Parents favored diaper brands that make a safe product for their baby (70 percent) and fit their baby well (60 percent). In contrast, only 22 percent care that the brand is environmentally responsible, declining by three percentage points over the last year.

Brands are challenged to communicate their commitment to sustainability

As sustainability is becoming a topic of growing interest, brands feel obliged to talk to their sustainability agenda and show their actions through initiatives and commitments to various time frames. Many brands aim to eventually become carbon neutral (offsetting one's emissions by planting trees), including

- Netflix by 2022
- Apple, Microsoft, and Facebook by 2030
- Amazon by 2040
- Coca-Cola and Nestlé by 2050
- Starbucks aimed to become "resource positive" by 2030, which it defines as reducing carbon emissions, water withdrawal, and waste by 50 percent while expanding plant-based menu options, shifting to reusable packaging, and investing in regenerative agricultural practices.

Brands rely on a range of terms to describe their sustainability initiatives, including but not limited to "carbon zero" (Hytch, a commuting app), "zero-carbon" (Zero Carbon Coffee), "climate positive" (Max Burgers), and even "air-made" (the carbon-neutral alcohol brand Air Vodka).

SPOTLIGHT ON | RUINART

Luxury products are often more durable than their cheaper alternatives. Further, they market timeless styles (think of the famous "Damier" from Louis Vuitton). Conversely, luxury brands are challenged to come up with sustainable offerings, as luxury does not intuitively associate with recyclable products.

LVMH-owned champagne house Ruinart recently unveiled its new eco-designed, recyclable packaging to demonstrate its commitment to social and environmental sustainability and support of more sustainable viticulture. The elegant packaging molded to the contours of the champagne bottle challenges conventional wisdom by exemplifying how recycling can convey luxury. This "second skin" is made of natural wood fibers and is nine times lighter than standard champagne packaging. Looking ahead, Maison Ruinart wants to demonstrate its commitment to more sustainable products, from tending vineyards through packaging to the consumer experience. Parent house Moët Hennessy also provides support and guidance to its partner winegrowers to convert to production methods that better respect the soil.[11]

Embracing sustainability

Being a "sustainable brand" has different meanings to different consumers:

Some brands are purposefully built around sustainability. Oatly was born sustainable. Its very existence is the manifestation of its mission. That is, support a systemic shift toward a sustainable food system and safeguard the planet for future generations.

Some brands have a purpose that aligns with sustainability:

Although denim is notorious for requiring large quantities of water to create jeans, Levi's new collection, Water<Less, uses 96 percent less water. Levi's implements sustainable practices through its entire design and manufacturing process and is working to source cotton that is 100 percent sustainable.

Some brands must shift to sustainability:

Volkswagen's mission is to power a grand switchover to electric vehicles and has enshrined the mission in VW's new tagline, "Way to Zero." They aim for total carbon neutrality by 2050, with the hope of creating a sustainable production process from design concept to showroom.

What to do next

Implementing sustainable practices is no easy feat and often takes years. The following are three examples of avenues you can explore straight away:

- How does my audience perceive my brand in terms of its sustainable and environmentally responsible practices?

- How prevalent is sustainability in the context of my specific markets, product categories, and competitor brands?

- What can I implement almost immediately that will improve the perception of my brand as it pertains to sustainability?

Using recycled materials, recyclable packaging, and starting a "gently used" program similar to IKEA, Levi's, and Lululemon all can help drive long-term perception.

Transparency

Burned by misleading claims, data breaches, supply chain issues, and counterfeit risk, consumers expect full transparency from brands across the value chain—how they source their products, their contribution to society and the economy, and their vision for the future. Further, brands are expected to reveal information about their prices, margins, operations, and financial statements. If brands refuse to provide these details, people will hunt for information elsewhere and can end up spreading negative information about the brand.

In contrast, brands that communicate transparently on production, costs, and even sensitive information increase consumers' perception of authenticity and drive trust as well as positive sentiment toward the brand.[12] Some brands even move toward "radical transparency," hoping to lure back disillusioned customers. For example, H&M-owned Arket lists where its products are made and shows pictures of the manufacturing floors.[13]

In the event of a crisis, brands must become transparent by responding immediately, admitting they are at fault and apologizing. In doing so, the brand will regain the trust of 90 percent of consumers as long as it takes steps to resolve the issue.[14] In a similar vein, San Francisco–based fashion apparel brand Everlane gives its customers access to insights into all its costs along with detailed information on the factory where its products are made.

In the long run, brands that refuse to become more transparent about their practices will suffer as consumers question what they have to hide. Admittedly, transparency is more challenging for some industries than for others. When an eight-story factory collapsed in Bangladesh in 2013, killing 1,134 people and injuring 2,500—the deadliest garment factory disaster in history[15]—it took several weeks for brands such as Benetton, Prada, Mango, and Walmart to understand why their labels had been found among the ruins. These brands rarely owned their manufacturing plants and relied on an opaque system of subcontractors and agents known as "indirect sourcing." This system often prevents brands from monitoring worker conditions.

This distrust extends to business leaders. A survey conducted by the *Financial Times* showed that just 15 percent of non-marketing business leaders saw a strong brand as important, and only 20 percent saw it as very important to increase profitability and deliver future cash flow.

Upcycling, recycling, and a product's renewed identity

Through recycling and upcycling, an old—and sometimes dysfunctional—product transforms into a new product with a clear past and present identity.

The past identity of the product is the starting point of its biographical story. From there, marketers can elaborate a narrative that describes the past identity of the product, which makes the product more meaningful to consumers. Note that the past function and identity of the product may not serve its current identity (for example, a worn-out airbag transformed into a backpack). Although this past identity is effectively useless, it supports the product's storytelling potential. Scholars coined this phenomenon "past identity salience."[16] These researchers highlight that storytelling products do not require an abundance of details. Rather, customers notice simple cues and then create their own stories.

Marketers can use these biographical stories, instead of creating stories about the product itself or the brand's value. For example, the Swiss brand Freitag highlights the fact that its bags and accessories are made of truck tarps; the Upcycling Deluxe store enables its customers to search for products based on what they used to be.

Repurposed products escape the stigma of the past because they have been transformed into something new. No matter how disgusting the product's past identity might be (a recycled tire or an old mosquito net), this "past identity salience" turns into a positive contribution to the product story. Research shows that in-store revenue more than quadruples when marketing touts the past identity of a product. Online "likes" for such upcycled products more than doubled, and upcycled products were chosen 12 percent more often when their past identities were prominently mentioned.

These unique, storied objects make their users feel special and allow people to create their own version of the product story.

The "right to repair" movement

Most of the goods we buy are designed to wear out, become obsolete, and look a bit uglier and less desirable to force us to replace them. The lifespan of many consumer products is controlled through tech interventions, a practice called "planned obsolescence."

Light bulbs, for example, could last for decades, as evidenced by the Centennial Light, a light bulb that is still shining after 120 years at a fire station in Livermore, California.[17] Such early incandescent light bulbs relied on a carbon filament eight times thicker than the more modern tungsten filament.[18]

As light bulbs became a mass-market commodity, brands figured they could drastically increase sales and profits by making light bulbs disposable. This led to the creation of the infamous "Phoebus Cartel" in 1924, the brainchild of light bulb manufacturers Osram (Germany), Associated Electrical Industries (United Kingdom), Philips (Netherlands), General

Electric (US), and La Compagnie des Lampes (France), which all colluded to cap light bulbs' lifetimes at 1,000 hours.[19]

Planned obsolescence then cropped up in other industries and now exists in various forms, such as repairs costing more than replacing products and aesthetic upgrades that relegate the older product versions as out of date or less stylish.

Batteries in smartphones, laptops, and other consumer electronics eventually die, hard drives run out of space, or operating systems can no longer be upgraded, forcing users to replace the product with a new one. One of the most obvious manifestations of planned obsolescence is in home printers, where microchips are programmed to prompt the user to replace ink cartridges that are not empty. Most recently, printer manufacturers lost cases to people claiming their "right to repair" and, in particular, the right to refill ink cartridges.[20]

Planned obsolescence is also damaging to the environment; we dispose of over 350 million ink cartridges a year, along with rare minerals mined to power our phones and laptops and highly polluting batteries.

The right to repair movement is gaining traction. The EU, UK, and US have enacted legislation that enables farmers to repair their tractors that were locked out by technology and directed the Federal Trade Commission to prevent manufacturers from enforcing repair restrictions.[21]

The right to repair movement stands for extending the life of products, making spare parts available, and legalizing repairs; repair cafés, Makers Labs, and community initiatives such as "The Restart Project" teach people to repair their broken electronics. The right to repair is a key tenet of the circular economy—one that relies on processes and economic activities that are regenerative or restorative by design.[22]

The end of planned obsolescence is an opportunity for brands

The new regulations and initiatives outlined above are expected to extend the life expectancy of white goods (dishwashers, toasters, and other countertop appliances) by up to 10 years.[23] Even brands unaffected by these regulations will need to transition, as product reviews from many publications now include sustainability ratings and influence consumer choice.

To harness the end of planned obsolescence, brands should

- Advertise the longevity of a product: Get ahead of the trend by taking a stance on longevity and sustainability, a tangible manifestation of brand purpose.

- Develop an ecosystem: A longer product life means a greater opportunity to keep customers in a brand ecosystem and sell companion products and services, such as subscriptions.

- Involve customers in the design process: Fashion apparel brand Freitag immerses its customers in the product creation process; customers choose the colors, materials, and patterns of their items in-store and create dummy templates the Freitag crew brings to life by sewing and riveting the materials while customers are watching.

- Offer special designs, repairs, and upgrades: These are all great means to generate store traffic. Once in-store, cross-sell and upsell other items and educate customers on how to use products.

Asphalte: Design, sell, and make

Asphalte is a French fashion brand whose business model relies on pre-ordering, meaning it produces only the clothes its audience demands and pre-purchases. Asphalte starts from the premise that we dispose of 60 percent of the clothes we buy within the first 12 months, either because these clothes are of poor quality or because we get tired of the design too quickly (or both). The fashion industry indirectly encourages this wasteful behavior. Fast-fashion retailers such as Zara and H&M brought us disposable clothing. Consequently, we now wear a given item about one-third fewer times than we did 15 years ago, making the fashion industry one of the largest polluters, accounting for 10 percent of global carbon emissions and 20 percent of global wastewater.[24] The clothing industry produces well over demand with the intent to sell inventory at a steep discount.

Asphalte proposes an alternative in producing clothes that are durable and timeless. It co-creates clothing items with its audience by asking people what clothes they need and will want to wear. When designing sneakers, for example, Asphalte asks participants when they wear the sneakers they already own, what they like and dislike about them, what colors and cloth they like the most, what stitching they prefer, and how much they'd be willing to spend. The questionnaire also challenges shoppers by asking them to consider a pair of sneakers at $99.

Asphalte develops just a few items. Their premise: A person is better off with one great sweater than five average ones. Pre-ordering also addresses production overflows, as Asphalte de facto sells everything it produces. Further, Asphalte doesn't store items, nor does it need to discount remnant inventory.

Recycling

Ipsos's studies show that consumers are concerned with the packaging of a product and the way it is disposed of when protecting the environment and adopting sustainable behaviors. That is, 56 percent of consumers are keen on avoiding products that have a lot of packaging, well ahead of other actions they could take to help protect the environment, such as not flying (43 percent) and eating fewer dairy products (36 percent).[25]

Recycling is by far the action that people believe is the most helpful for the environment,[26] even though the actual positive impact of recycling product packaging is much lower than avoiding long-distance flights or not having a car.[27] Therefore, brands invest heavily in recyclable packaging, as it is the most impactful and likely the easiest sustainability-related initiative they can implement. Among the most innovative brands, Nespresso provides its users with bags to store used capsules they can ship back to stores at no charge. Also, cooking school Haven's Kitchen offers its signature sauces in 100 percent recyclable pouches. On a larger scale, Colgate has redesigned its toothpaste tubes so that they can now be recycled in curbside bins. The brand expects all tubes in its portfolio to be recyclable by 2025, although Colgate will likely need to educate its customers on recycling the tubes after decades of throwing these tubes in the trash.[28]

Compostable packaging

No Evil Foods packages its products with fully compostable materials. The brand also partners with nonprofit organizations to reclaim plastic waste that would otherwise be landfilled, burned, or flushed into waterways. Kencko aims to make fruit and vegetables more accessible with its just-add-water mixes of freeze-dried fruit/vegetable powders. The brand has phased out conventional single-use plastics in favor of fully compostable packets (made from plants) to minimize its footprint. In a similar vein, chocolate and granola brand Alter Eco's pouches use non-toxic ink, eucalyptus, birch, and a layer of non-GMO corn.

Reduce, reuse, recycle programs

Beyond packaging-related initiatives, an increasing number of brands implement programs that involve their customers and generate store traffic while doing good for the environment and the local community.

In the food and beverage arena, Good Culture proposes cottage cheese that is good for people, the animals, and the environment by investing in family farms to elevate animal care and well-being, land stewardship, and milk quality. Also, Dash Water infuses its waters with "wonky fruits," ones that stores and consumers would reject because they are bent or somewhat misshapen.

With its "Back to M·A·C" program, M·A·C Cosmetics encourages its customers to return containers and receive a free M·A·C lipstick. In line with this initiative, Body Shop gives away $5 gift vouchers to shoppers who return and refill their pots and bottles. Cosmetic retailer Lush rewards customers with a free, fresh face mask when they return five clean, empty pots to a store.[29]

Patagonia's "Buy Less Demand More" initiative offers used goods alongside brand-new products on its website.

Recommerce

As consumers demand more sustainable products and practices, brands must embrace and propel recommerce, the selling of previously owned products that buyers reuse, recycle, repair, or resell. Recommerce is predicted to account for 14 percent of the footwear, apparel, and accessories market by 2024, up from 7 percent in 2020. Apparel resales alone could become a $64 billion market by 2024.[30] By 2025, recommerce is projected to grow 11 times faster than the broader retail clothing sector.[31]

According to the World Economic Forum, clothing production has roughly doubled since 2000 and shoppers keep their garments for only half as long as they used to. The silver lining is millennials and Gen Z are value-driven consumers who prefer to buy from brands that engage in sustainable practices. Some even shop exclusively for secondhand apparel, allowing them to wear higher-quality garments they couldn't otherwise afford while minimizing their carbon footprint and reinforcing their social credentials.

Early movers in the recommerce space were marketplaces such as The RealReal and Poshmark, along with peer-to-peer resale platforms like Depop. Name brands are starting to respond, working with logistics providers that help set up their resale market operations. As such, the Renewal Workshop takes damaged and returned inventory from retailers and turns it into renewed products that are then sold through brand-owned websites or shared marketplaces. It provides technology and logistics to its brand partners such as Carhartt, The North Face, Prada, and PEARL iZUMi. Further, it accumulates data on items that flow through its system and shares this data with brands to help them improve the design and production of future clothing lines. For example, fashion brand Fendi relaunched its signature monogram print "Zucca" as it noticed a surge in demand for vintage, preowned Fendi garments in the iconic print.[32] The same can be said of Dior's vintage "saddle" bag, which is going through a revival 20 years after it made its debut under John Galliano.[33]

The circular economy

Our rate of consumption has increased fourfold since 1970 while the population has only doubled. In contrast with the linear economy where we produce, consume, and dispose of goods, the circular economy proposes to extract fewer raw materials and reuse the ones we have already extracted. It is a framework to tackle global challenges such as waste, pollution, and biodiversity. This framework involves not only recycling but also remanufacturing, refurbishing, reusing, and repairing by sourcing energy through product production, distribution, usage, and disposal.

Over the next few years, consumers will likely be drawn to a circular economy for its convenience; a circular economy enables consumers to put a product back into the supply chain as a "rent, recycle, or resell" product. Today, only 9 percent of our economy is circular, making the circular economy possibly the biggest transformation companies will embark on since the Industrial Revolution.

Rent: It's cheaper

In more and more categories, people choose to rent rather than own goods. Besides our growing concern for the environment, this trend is bolstered by social media: our posts on Instagram and other platforms often depict an idealized lifestyle captured with a picture or a short video that does not require owning anything but only using it for a few minutes. Conversely, younger consumers who live through social media are hungry for newness.

Brands like Spotify, Netflix, and Zipcar have helped demonstrate the benefits of rentals as consumers have realized that there was a limited upside to owning a CD, DVD, or even a car. This new mindset is propelling the success of rental and preowned businesses such as Rent the Runway, which rents fashionable outfits, and The RealReal, which sells gently used luxury brands. In China, YCloset operates a subscription model in which customers access a range of clothing and accessories for a flat monthly fee. We will also increasingly seek "rental native" brands, created exclusively to be rented or accessed through subscription models.

Recommerce as a new model for brand engagement

Recommerce offers new opportunities for brand engagements. Brands can extend their relationships with existing customers and foster new ones with shoppers who might not have otherwise purchased items at full price. Indeed, 50 percent of recommerce shoppers try a new brand,[34] offering companies a chance to capture a younger and less affluent audience. As such, recommerce is a cost-effective channel to acquire new customers and extend customer lifetime value with brand loyalists.

That said, authenticating products is a major challenge for marketplaces, consumers, and brands alike. Lawsuits between secondary marketplaces and brands have outlined the issue; brands argue that these marketplaces cannot guarantee the authenticity of products without the input of brands themselves. Ultimately, this erodes consumer trust and negatively impacts items, prices, and margins.

To address this challenge, the World Economic Forum is leading an initiative that enables brands to attach a digital identifier to their products (for example, a unique QR code displayed on the label of the item). This identifier enables the brand to authenticate an item instantly as the product finds its way to a recommerce platform. This "certification" model is similar to the role Visa and Mastercard play in authenticating and securing payment transactions. In the long run, it offers a scalable way for brands to sell their items through recommerce. World Retail Congress

Chairman Ian McGarrigle notes that "digitization is what allows brands to track the life cycle of a product, which is a building block of the circular economy."[35]

This QR code also enables consumers to learn about the provenance of products, from the farm where the cotton was harvested and the factory where the garment was manufactured. In the meantime, recommerce platforms like Grailed rely on in-house moderators to screen digital listings, while the company Mercari uses photos to authenticate items.

Overall, recommerce presents a unique opportunity for brands to address their customers' sustainability concerns while protecting their brand identity, gathering data to inform research and development, generating additional profits, and increasing customer lifetime value. Furniture brand IKEA is one of the pioneers of recommerce. Through its "Buyback & Resell" service, IKEA allows customers to sell back their gently used IKEA furniture in exchange for a store credit. The goal is to provide a more affordable and sustainable way to acquire furniture.

For Jennifer Keesson, country sustainability manager for IKEA US, the firm is "passionate about making sustainable living easy and affordable for the many, and want to be part of a future that's better for both people and the planet."[36]

KEY TAKEAWAYS

- Consumer spending in the United States is at an all-time high; goods have become cheaper and we can shop online 24/7 without having to comply with restrictive store hours.

- We consume all these goods because marketing convinces us they make us happy, loved, and esteemed, but too many products make us feel happy one moment and miserable the next.

- Consumers influence business decisions by which brand they buy, based on its environmental impact.

- Brands feel obliged to talk to their sustainability agenda and show their actions through initiatives and commitments to various time frames.

- Consumers expect full transparency from brands across the value chain and to understand how brands source their products, their contribution to society and the economy, and their vision for the future.

- In the long run, brands that refuse to become more transparent about their practices will suffer as consumers question what they have to hide.

- Recycling and upcycling transform a product; it is given a clear past and present identity.

- Repurposed products escape the stigma of the past because they have been transformed into something new.

- Combating planned obsolescence, the "right to repair" movement is gaining traction as we become increasingly concerned with the downsides of consumerism, including its environmental impact.

- Brands can also address the demand for more sustainable products and practices through recommerce, the selling of previously owned products that buyers reuse, recycle, repair, or resell.

THE ASSEMBLERS

The artists we admire the most are talented, but not always in the way we may think. Their real talent is often *assembling* to deliver their artistic vision, rather than necessarily creating the work of art.

They can teach us how to cope with our impostor syndrome and create and market brands at scale.

What Picasso knew and all marketers need to learn

In the early 1900s, artists from all over Europe congregated in Montmartre, a community made of cobbled streets, vineyards, and windmills on the outskirts of Paris. There, these impoverished artists lived a bohemian ideal, gathering in low-rent ateliers to create "art for art's sake." Among these artists was Pablo Picasso, whose goal was to "live like a pauper, but with plenty of money." Picasso knew he was a great painter but realized his talent wouldn't be enough. He had to create an aura to prompt fascination and intrigue beyond his art.

Throughout his career, Picasso worked tirelessly on his art and on establishing his brand. First, he changed his name from Pablo Ruiz to Pablo Picasso and finally to just Picasso, becoming the first artist known only by a single name well before Cher, Madonna, or Zendaya.

Picasso also knew he needed a wide range of products to sell. He produced an estimated 50,000 pieces of artwork during his lifetime, from paintings and drawings to sculptures and ceramics. Picasso worked closely with art merchants to gain exposure, monitor competition, and restrain distribution.

Picasso not only created art for art's sake; he produced work that was highly differentiated and would endure. By his death in 1973, Picasso had achieved name recognition of around 95 percent in most countries[1] and his net worth was estimated at $500 million. Today, Picasso's art is no longer exclusive to a handful of rich collectors; it exists through mugs, T-shirts, tableware, and even in a song by hip-hop artist Jay-Z.

The dominance of intellectual elites is over

Unarguably, Picasso was an extremely talented, prolific, and visionary artist. However, at the time, creating, marketing, and even enjoying the arts was limited to a handful of artists, merchants, and collectors; an elite group of connoisseurs determined what art was "important," created scarcity, and fostered exclusion by limiting access to both artists and their audiences.

Today, the dominance of this intellectual elite is over. Thanks to technology and digital media, we are now *all* creators, curators, collectors, and marketers. There is only one Picasso, but we are all artists.

To their credit, these elites discovered and propelled talents such as Picasso, Fernand Léger, and, more recently, Jeff Koons, Damien Hirst, and numerous others. "What would have become of us if Kahnweiler hadn't had a business sense?," Picasso said of his gallerist Daniel-Henry Kahnweiler.[2]

But times have changed. While a microscopic community of collectors still spends millions at auction houses, the arts are no longer constrained to a single standard of quality. New media provides us with a platform for creating, viewing, and sharing art on an unprecedented scale. Film, short videos, and video games are now seen as culturally and artistically relevant as traditional arts such as theater, painting, and opera.

That said, the democratization of art does not take anything away from traditional institutions. It is exactly the opposite: conscious that a six-inch screen doesn't do the arts justice, digital media drives people to see the original artwork. American museums are evolving their offerings to stay current by delivering immersive experiences that bring together visual arts, technology, and performances. Museums are visited approximately 850 million times each year, more than the attendance for all theme parks and sporting events combined.[3]

The same goes for advertising and branding. The advertising industry owes a lot to the original "mad men" who ruled Madison Avenue in the late 1950s. The likes of David Ogilvy, Bill Bernbach, and George Lois brought the power of creativity and storytelling to advertising. However, Ogilvy reckoned that senior advertising executives and creative directors did not have a monopoly on great advertising; junior employees, researchers, and everyday people were just as capable of coming up with big ideas.

Pharrell Williams

In 2015, Marvin Gaye's family sued music star and 13-time Grammy Award winner Pharrell Williams and singer Robin Thicke for copyright infringement over their hit single "Blurred Lines." In April 2014, lawyers for Gaye's estate held an awkward, nerve-wracking deposition with Williams, repeatedly asking him to read music:[4]

What are the chords in a 12-bar blues?

I'm not here to teach you music.

Does the answer mean you don't know?

I don't know.

You've not received any college or formal education with respect to music, correct?

No, sir.

Can you read musical notation?

Yes, sir.

Can you write in musical notation?

No.

Can you read pitches in musical notation?

No.

A report was put before Williams and he was asked to look at it.

What are the names of those notes?

I'm not comfortable with this.

What is the duration of those notes?

I'm not comfortable.

[. . .] What are the names and duration of those notes?

I can't answer you at this time.

I'm just asking you if you can read notes. You told me you could, and you can't do it can you?

I'm not comfortable.

And that's because you actually can't read musical notes, can you?

I'm not comfortable.

The deposition implies that Pharrell Williams is one of many artists who doesn't know or practice their art. Chef Alain Ducasse, who operates over 70 establishments around the world, hasn't cooked for years. Annie Leibovitz admits she is not a "technical photographer"; she shoots pictures with rudimentary lighting and staging. Michelangelo, Lichtenstein, and Warhol had extensive teams of collaborators helping to produce their art at scale; Warhol's studio was called The Factory. The same is true of Koons, Hirst, and other successful artists today who, along with entrepreneurs and brand managers, are most often assemblers, producers, and visionaries who rely on their instinct over data.

What marketers can learn from DJ Khaled

Khaled Mohammed Khaled, known as DJ Khaled, started his career at the music shop Odyssey Records as a teen in New Orleans before making his way to Miami to eventually become a DJ at station WEDR. Just like Ducasse doesn't cook, DJ Khaled allegedly hasn't scratched records for years, nor does he produce his own beats. His main talents are coming up with ideas, bringing the right people to his ideas, and leading the entire production process.

DJ Khaled is credited on most songs as an artist even though he has no production credits and minimal vocal appearances on any of his records. He is a relentless promoter, getting the word out for his artists (insert social media following here). He also surrounds himself with successful artists who appeal to a slightly different audience: Lil Wayne, Kanye West, and Jennifer Lopez.

"There are beat-makers and there are producers," Khaled said. "I'm a producer. I put together amazing records, whether that's finding the beat or putting the right hook on there, and picking the right artists on the record.

That's me being an A&R (artist and repertoire) and I'm making sure that they give me their best. A Khaled record is always the best."[5]

DJ Khaled embraced sonic branding in his first album in 2006 and has developed a multitude of audio tags. Sonic branding, also referred to as audio branding, is creating a brand identity through sound. DJ Khaled's primary audio tags are[6] "DJ Khaled," "Anotha One," and "We the Best" (sometimes modified to "We the Best Music"). He explains:

> "We the best" is who we are. It's like Nike's "Just do it."
> We the best over here. It's a music company, it's a char-
> ity, it's what we represent, it's who we are, and it's what
> we are here to motivate and inspire the young world.[7]

Artists operate factories and follow a template

Artists were seen as skilled laborers as far back as ancient Egypt in 2500 BCE. It was in the fifteenth century during the Italian Renaissance that these craftsmen transitioned to artists. Da Vinci, Botticelli, Del Verrocchio, and many others had assistants to help produce high-quantity and high-quality art. Having an assistant wasn't frowned upon and did not diminish the reputation of these masters. As demand grew, they had to exponentially increase their production and their assistants became instrumental in the art-making process. Rubens, for example, produced up to two paintings a week to satisfy overwhelming demand from the clergy and aristocracy. If more than 1,500 are attributed to Rubens, his assistants did most of the work by copying sketches the master had drafted. In many of his paintings, Rubens only contributed finishing touches and his signature.

Modern art, like many other billion-dollar industries, relies heavily on outsourced physical labor and industrialized production. Koons does not produce any of his work himself but employs a large team in New York's Hudson Yards that produces his designs. Recently, he went one step further by laying off three-quarters of his assistants. Embracing technology just like any other enterprise, Koons relies on advanced software programs and a small team of programmers and engineers to model his sculptures. The manufacturing process is then outsourced to 12 machines that do most of the carving for him.[8]

> It's a machine that produces reality.
>
> —OLAFUR ELIASSON ON HIS STUDIO,
> WHERE UP TO 90 EMPLOYEES DESIGN,
> PRODUCE, AND MARKET HIS ART

No, not all artists are starving

The cliché of the poor, starving artist is a romantic ideology that is mostly untrue. At the onset of the Industrial Revolution, art and culture were the exclusivity of the wealthy (factory owners, merchants . . .), as they had more time and resources to learn and access art. Meanwhile, workers spent their time on the factory floors. The advent of printing, photographic and cinematographic technologies enabled the mass production of culture. Then, cultural consumption got separated between popular culture that the masses consumed passively (movies, pictures) and the high art that heightened the senses.[9] This dichotomy set the tone for the articulation of creativity through most of the twentieth century: artists produced art for the elites—the rest was art in industrialized forms produced by Hollywood studios.

The arts enable the creation of powerful and purposeful brands

The arts, through culture and creativity, help brands to stand out, con-nect with their audience on an emotional level, and do good for our society. When PepsiCo decided to create a new brand of premium water, it introduced LIFEWTR, a bottle with an eclectic and colorful label designed by emerging artists. To tie together marketing, brand purpose, and philanthropy, PepsiCo's LIFEWATR supports a $100,000 annual fund for the Brooklyn Museum and donates art supplies to pub-lic schools.

LIFEWATR is just one example of how the arts are pervasive in branding across numerous categories. Although luxury brands like BMW and Louis Vuitton have long collaborated with artists, the rise of social media and the blending of pop culture with contemporary art has accel-erated alliances between artists and mainstream brands. Japanese casual wear designer Uniqlo collaborates with emerging tastemakers in art, film, and interior design. New artists feature their work on its T-shirts, and Uniqlo sponsors a grant for public artwork in New York City.

Brand artists' collaborations span many industries. In high fashion, Calvin Klein enlisted artist Sterling Ruby to redesign its flagship stores in Paris and Manhattan. In technology, Adobe, Kickstarter, and Facebook host artist-in-residence programs in their offices. Even dating industry giant OkCupid retained Maurizio Cattelan and his collaborator Pierpaolo Ferrari to create an ad campaign based on the duo's surrealist imagery. The campaign reclaims the initials DTF ("Down To F**k") and replaces the invitation for sex with nonsexual activities and interests such as "fighting about the president" or "finishing a novel."[10]

By blending art and marketing, these projects created unique brands and products that stand out. In the short run, they spark a conversation among consumers, art enthusiasts, and marketers. These projects also receive extensive media coverage, which far outweighs the costs involved in creating campaigns. In the long run, the arts enable brands to become classics, transcending the test of time and generations.

To survive and thrive, brands can no longer merely market products that are culturally relevant or repackage the cultural content others create—they need to become artistic and cultural agents. They must become a legitimate form of expressive art and culture.

How the arts benefit both brands and consumers

Artful housewares, furniture, and accessories were once exclusive to upscale brands like Alessi, Kartell, or Knoll. Today, art is entering the life of everyday people. Brands like Nike, Uniqlo, and IKEA have made art and design accessible to the masses.

The same goes for the service industry. Originally, globally renowned artists like Olivia Steele, Takashi Murakami, and Damien Hirst catered to select galleries, auction houses, and collectors. Now, their art helped turn the Palms Casino Resort in Las Vegas from a decrepit hotel off the strip into a destination for leisure travelers. The hotel commissioned these artists to create a collection of bold, relevant, and interactive pieces to give guests a one-of-a-kind experience from the casino gaming floors to the mini-bar.

Collaborations between artists and brands make the arts accessible and visible for much longer than if they were exhibited at galleries or museums.

Art promotes well-being

Art is a form of consumption that has a positive, lasting impact on us. Whether it is a song, a photograph, a painting, a movie, a spatiotemporal experiment, or a good advertisement, art transports us to a new place while being rooted in the physical experience of our bodies. It evokes emotions and feelings over function, but art does not tell us what to do; it connects us to our senses, body, and mind. "Art makes the world felt," says Olafur Eliasson, "and this felt feeling may spur thinking, engagement, and even action."[11]

Art, creativity, design, and culture also benefit our professional life. In the next few years, AI and machine learning will replace millions of bookkeeping clerks, market research analysts, and telemarketers. The bright spot is that machines cannot be trained to be creative—big ideas and critical thinking remain exclusive to humans. Art and creativity empower indispensability for employees and brands.

Art is engaging and connects us

Art celebrates imagination, provokes inspiration, and fosters community. Art has helped people navigate their differences, validate their self-worth, and process deep tragedies. Research shows that art education helps at-risk teenagers and young adults improve their academic achievements and promote social engagement. Indeed, art and culture bring people together to share an experience, even if they see the world in different ways.

Snoop Dogg and Martha Stewart

At first sight, Snoop Dogg and Martha Stewart have little in common, but they have evolved their brands via two seasons of their cooking show, *Martha & Snoop's Potluck Dinner Party*. It's a perfect example of assemblage. Snoop Dogg helped transform Martha Stewart's personal brand from being America's most earnest homemaker into "America's cool weed Grandma."[12] The show's stunts include Martha wearing a blinged-out cheese grater necklace, drinking out of a pimp cup, and claiming to enjoy Snoop Dogg's smokes. Snoop Dogg enables Martha Stewart to stay relevant and connect with a younger audience that wouldn't watch her Thanksgiving leftover recipes, let alone buy her gadgets and cookbooks.[13]

Stewart helped Snoop Dogg become a more family-friendly figure. Before partnering with her, Snoop Dogg's music and personal brand catered to hip-hop devotees, regular cannabis consumers, and a few other niche audiences. Considering his gangsta rapper image and that he did jail time for drug offenses, Snoop Dogg wasn't, by conventional standards, a role model.

Recently, the duo partnered with lighter company BIC to playfully promote how people can use BIC'S EZ Reach lighters. In the ad, marijuana aficionado Snoop Dogg finds Stewart smoking a turkey, which she lit with her BIC lighter. "Martha, I didn't know you was into this," says Snoop. The pair then shows how the lighter is perfect for lighting candles and lanterns before deciding to use it for their "favorite activity" of roasting marshmallows over a bonfire.[14]

"Snoop Dogg and Martha Stewart allow us to connect with our consumers in a relevant and playful way while highlighting all the usage occasions and core benefits that set EZ Reach apart in the lighter category,"[15] said Mary Fox, general manager of BIC North America.

Cameo, or the illusion of befriending the stars

Before the advent of social media, we adored the likes of Brooke Shields, George Clooney, Brad Pitt, and Madonna from afar. These personalities were not relatable or accessible; hidden in their penthouses and Hollywood mansions, their day-to-day lifestyle had little in common with ours. Enter social media personalities and "influencers," whose primary function is to reduce social distance. Videos depict them as the girl/guy next door and they often are reachable via direct message. While mostly harmless, this proximity is an illusion. Influencers have become celebrities in their own right, complete with agents, talent managers, lawyers, and production crews that help script, shoot, and edit their "candid" videos.

Cameo, an app that seemingly gives us the best of both worlds, creates "authentic fan connections" with "tens of thousands of stars." For $25 to $2,500, fans can have the celebrity of their choice congratulate them on their graduation, give them a personal birthday greeting, or even engage in a live conversation. This cameo appearance is delivered to the fan within a few days or even hours.

Perhaps the most interesting (or most telling) section on Cameo is "Politics," where one can connect with the personalities including Michael Cohen, Rudy Giuliani, Roger Stone, and Rod Blagojevich.

SPOTLIGHT ON | SONG CANDY

Song Candy is a first-of-its-kind specialized agency that develops breakthrough music-driven campaigns and custom branded music for TikTok, Instagram, YouTube, Spotify, and more. It combines data science, music, and marketing to create music-driven campaigns engineered to be memorable and shareable.

Gabbie Bradford, a co-founder of Song Candy, reflected on her previous agency experience, noting:

> In the past, agencies have been making posts but overlooked sound. We would buy $100 in stock music . . . But what struck me is music has always been part of advertising. And it then fades away with social media. Now, brands are thinking about music again.

TikTok is a sound-centric experience and has become a place for people to discover new music. "You cannot really enjoy that platform without music," noted Bradford. The opportunity is for brands to "tell the brand story but in a way that is a song you want to listen to and add to your playlist." And hopefully, the song will get stuck in our heads, an earworm.

Over the last ten years, brands shifted toward creating content and now make movies (think of *The Lego Movie*) and books (Weber Grill's *Weber's Greatest Hits*). Bradford said music is another avenue brands can pursue.

> Brands should create music at the same caliber artists are. As brands want to foster deeper connections and loyalty, music is such a powerful tool: it creates connection and memories that get us back to a time like prom and wedding day.

Music is five times more memorable than visuals: Sounds mark us for five seconds; images leave our minds in less than a second.[16]

Song Candy prides itself in creating music that sticks. To come up with these earworms, it has created a playbook that defines the specific qualities the song must have: a simple melody, lots of repetition, and certain keys.

When engaging with a brand client, Song Candy narrows down the type of emotions the brand intends to convey through its "musical mood board," an interactive and collaborative platform hosted on its website.

Song Candy also tracks the most popular songs on TikTok and Apple Music, particularly songs that are most popular with the target audience of their brand clients. Song Candy then uses these songs as an inspiration for musical direction and even distributes the song on platforms like TikTok so that people can search for the song and create content for it, in turn generating word of mouth for the brand.

KEY TAKEAWAYS ✶ ✶ ✶

- Picasso knew he was a great painter but realized his talent wouldn't be enough. He had to create an aura to prompt fascination and intrigue beyond his art. He marketed his art by branding his name and producing work that was differentiated across a wide range of products.

- The dominance of the intellectual elite is over. Thanks to technology and digital media, all of us are creators, curators, collectors, and marketers.

- Senior advertising executives and creative directors do not have a monopoly on great marketing; junior employees, researchers, and everyday people are just as capable of coming up with big ideas.

- Pharrell Williams appears to be one of the artists who doesn't really either know or practice their art. Chef Alain Ducasse hasn't cooked for years. Annie Leibovitz admits she is not a "technical photographer."

- DJ Khaled embraced sonic branding from his first album in 2006 and has developed a multitude of audio tags. Sonic branding, or audio branding, is creating a brand identity through sound.

- Modern art, like many other billion-dollar industries, relies heavily on outsourced physical labor and industrialized production.

- The arts, through culture and creativity, help brands stand out, connect with their audience on an emotional level, and do good for our society.

- Brand–artist collaboration spans many industries, including high fashion, technology, and even match-making.

- To survive and thrive, brands need to become artistic and cultural agents.

- Artful housewares, furniture, and accessories are no longer exclusive to upscale brands; Nike, Uniqlo, and IKEA have made art and design accessible to the masses.

NOW, IT IS YOUR TURN

It is your turn to make a positive impact on your community and the world. No matter your background, education, and professional achievements, you are capable of great things. Statistically, 99 percent of us did not go to the top 1 percent of schools, have famous parents, or a hefty trust fund. Yet we can all become successful in our own right by making the most of what we have and taking small steps. We don't have to succeed immediately, but we owe it to ourselves to try. In its campaign "Play New," Nike encourages people to try without worrying about success. The spot shows athletes trying sports they are not known for while a voice-over says, "Here's to going for it . . . and being terrible. Here's to giving it a shot, even though your shot is garbage." The spot concludes with "You know what doesn't suck? Trying to do something you've never done before."[1]

I hope *Assemblage* inspires you to be creative, try new things, and take risks. Here is some parting advice on how to manifest this.

To be creative, stop googling things

"The best place to hide a dead body is page two of Google search results," because a whopping 95 percent of all online searches stop at page one's results. And when browsing through page one, we only care about what's at the top; the first organic result on that page captures about 32.5 percent of overall search traffic. The second result sees 17.6 percent; the seventh, only 3.5 percent.[2] Further, search engines and media outlets tailor search results based on users' previous searches and website visitation—that's how different users access different results. Eli Pariser coined this phenomenon the "filter bubble," which prevents us from being exposed to content that could broaden or challenge our views. We don't decide what gets in our bubble and don't see what is filtered out.

Break free from the harmonization of taste

We're overly reliant on the internet for inspiration, which has greatly homogenized people's tastes across the world. On the one hand, digital platforms like Pinterest have made it easier than ever to search for trends in coffee shops, for example. On the other hand, such searches reveal that all coffee shops look the same; whether in New York, Los Angeles, Chicago, or London, most independent coffee shops have adopted the same faux-artisanal aesthetic with exposed brick, raw wood tables, and hanging Edison bulbs. The same goes for start-up offices, which often rely on minimalist furniture, industrial lighting, and reclaimed wood. Writer and critic Kyle Chayka calls this phenomenon "AirSpace,"[3] the confluence of style in the physical world created by online technology. "The connective emotional grid of social media platforms is what drives the impression of AirSpace," Chayka argues. "If taste is globalized, then the logical endpoint is a world in which aesthetic diversity decreases."

Sell your brand by telling people not to buy it

We are not perfect and neither are the brands we buy. Counterintuitively, many brands have succeeded by revealing their flaws or admitting flat out that they are not the best. Perhaps what is most important is to strive to improve. In the 1960s, car rental company Avis had trailed Hertz, its key competitor, since Avis's inception. Ad agency Doyle Dane Bernbach decided to embrace Avis's second-place status and created the "We try harder" campaign. The ads are credited with finally making Avis profitable.[4]

More recently, Carlsberg evolved its tagline from "Probably the best beer in the world" to "Probably not the best beer in the world" after research showed that Carlsberg was underperforming compared with its competitors. Based on this research, it improved its product and reintroduced the lager as "rebrewed from head to toe," accompanied by the hashtag #newbrew, "in pursuit of better beer."

> **It is not how good you are; it's how good you want to be.**
> —PAUL ARDEN

Some brands even exaggerate their flaws to humor their audience. To promote their new Las Vegas show, magicians Penn & Teller once claimed the tagline, "Fewer audience injuries than last year!"[5] In a similar vein, marketing author Christopher Lochhead created an ad for his podcast that showcased a review from *The Economist* calling the podcast "off-putting to some," along with reviews from Lochhead's listeners: "annoying host," "uses profanity needlessly," "very disappointing."

Risk extending your brand

While many marketers are terrified to extend their brand beyond its core product, the risks associated with such an endeavor are often overstated. Indeed, a failed extension is unlikely to damage the flagship brand in the long run. Besides, risk conveys authenticity and mistakes can help make the brand more authentic.

Virgin once entertained the arcane idea to displace Coke and Pepsi with its Virgin Cola. By now, almost everyone has forgotten about the failed cola. However, many remember the stunts of Virgin founder Richard Branson. Most recently, they likely remember that Branson was the first civilian to go to space.

Ferrari released a "Scuderia Ferrari Forte," a cheap, unrefined cologne for men. Even if the fragrance fails, it is unlikely Ferrari enthusiasts will ever question the Stallion's ability to build a race car just because it could not come up with a decent perfume. Ferrari's car shipments grew 22 percent in 2021 and were up 10 percent in 2019.[6] Car manufacturers can (seemingly) also risk their brand when expanding in new automotive categories. When Porsche started marketing SUVs, many thought it would lead to the demise of the core brand image centered around the 911, a sporty, upmarket car. Today, Porsche's SUVs are the manufacturer's best sellers, broadening the appeal of the brand to well-to-do family suburbanites; the move did not dent the appeal of its sports cars.

Struggling British retailer John Lewis plans on building 10,000-plus homes within its existing land footprint.[7] A retailer getting into real estate makes complete sense. The department stores are struggling; in 2021, the retailer posted a £648 million loss and closed one-third of its retail network as the pandemic and Amazon decimated its business. Most department stores like John Lewis in the UK and Macys and Nordstrom in the US will never recover; they are too big to deliver a personal experience but too small to compete with Amazon on assortment. The bottom line is John Lewis will die if it stays focused on its core business.

Although its stores are struggling, John Lewis remains one of the most recognized and trusted brands in UK retail. This brand equity will carry over to John Lewis's property venture.

Most publicity is good publicity

Kärcher is a German family-owned company that makes high-pressure cleaners, among other cleaning equipment. In 2005, French interior minister Nicolas Sarkozy suggested cleaning out France's infamous suburbs with a Kärcher. In January 2022, Republican presidential candidate Valérie Pécresse suggested "bring[ing] out the Kärcher again" after two presidents "put it away in the cellar for more than 10 years." Ever since Sarkozy used the brand name as a metaphor for solving tensions in France's rough suburbs, Kärcher has tried to convince French politicians to stop using its name in the context of civil unrest and immigration. In January 2022, Kärcher again asked politicians and the media to stop "any use of its name in the sphere of policy which damages its brand and the values of the company."

While the brand tries to come across as indignant, this sudden exposure is a blessing in disguise. First, because the Kärcher brand was front and center in virtually all French news outlets for two days, it offered a kind of brand exposure money can't buy. For the last 40 years, Kärcher has been running a global campaign to clean historical monuments such as the Obelisk in Paris, France, and the Avicii Arena in Stockholm, Sweden.[8] While well-meaning, hardly anyone sees or remembers the campaign. In contrast, Google trends show that searches for Kärcher jumped 108 percent after Pécresse mentioned the brand.[9] As controversial as the metaphor might be, it highlights the main functional feature of the product. That is, Kärcher does a great job at cleaning dirt.

Tackle taboos

Many of the causes that Benetton championed in the 1980s have gained wider acceptance today. However, our society overall (and by extension, marketers, most of whom tend to follow the flock rather than challenging anything) still feels uneasy with topics like sex, death, and mental health. For example, life insurance and funeral companies' marketing is most often bland, approaching these subjects with cautious tones and one-size-fits-all stock footage. Still, some brands dare to challenge this status quo with provocative, yet appropriate messaging.

- Zacherl Funeral Home in Fond du Lac, Wisconsin, launched a billboard campaign aimed at youth safety—avoiding traffic fatalities, drug overdoses, and teen suicide. The billboard features a coffin adorned with a spray of red roses. The tagline reads, "You don't want to be ordering these flowers for prom. Be safe. We can wait."[10]

- DeadHappy is a life insurance company that suggests its customers "make a death wish." The website says, "Not the desire for self-annihilation, but our way of helping you to express what you want to happen when you die."[11]

By harnessing these difficult topics, brands and advertising executives have an opportunity to positively affect society, not just sell products.

- In the UK, suicide is the biggest killer of men under 50.[12] In response, Campaign Against Living Miserably (CALM) aims to combat male suicide by "standing against feeling like shit, standing up to stereotypes, and standing together to show life is always worth living."[13]

- Recycled toilet paper brand Who Gives a Crap donates 50 percent of its profits to WaterAid, acknowledging that more people in the world have access to a mobile phone than to a toilet.[14]

- Hair removal brand Treatwell has partnered with Public Health England to promote cervical cancer screenings. While the brand has seen a sharp increase of women booking waxing appointments (up 84 percent from 2019), the number of women attending their cervical screenings is at a 20-year low; 25 percent don't go.[15]

How brands can tackle taboos:

- Use the same words and expressions as the public. By naming its brand "Who Gives a Crap," the toilet paper company establishes proximity and empathy with its audience.

- Be bold. Taglines such as the ones from Zacherl Funeral Home and DeadHappy won't please everyone. Partner with a government agency or charity and share a significant portion of your profit. The investment will more than pay for itself; your partner will bring to your brand the credibility and visibility it couldn't achieve on its own.

We don't have to reinvent the wheel

It would be pretentious, even fraudulent, to claim that marketing management frameworks (or even the broader lifestyle ones) that surround us today are new. Obsessed with predicting the future, today's so-called visionaries and thought leaders tend to ignore or conveniently forget what the past brought us. Bestselling author Daniel Pink said, "looking backward moves us forward." Rather than necessarily trying to reinvent the wheel, it is often more efficient and effective to revisit learnings from the past and adapt them to the current environment.

- Delivering an immersive experience in commerce in general and retail, in particular, is positioned by many (including myself) as the way to grow (and frankly, salvage) physical retail. Note that the concept of delivering "extraordinary experiences" that provide absorption, integration, personal control, new perceptions, joy, and spontaneity was first theorized by researchers Eric Arnould and Linda Price in an academic journal—in 1993.[16]

- The concepts of aesthetic consumerism that govern Instagram (described in Chapter 1) were outlined by photographer Susan Sontag—in 1977.

- Purpose-led advertising surfaced in the 1980s through the campaigns of fashion brand Benetton, well before "brand purpose" became the obsession it is today.

And the list goes on.

We have to do the right thing—for people and the world

As I write this book in April 2022, Russia is invading Ukraine, claiming thousands of lives, and has displaced over 1.5 million people. Most of the international community responded to this invasion with stringent sanctions against Russia and oligarchs close to President Vladimir Putin, who enjoy a luxurious lifestyle in and outside of their country.

In response to this crisis, the advertising industry took a stance on the conflict, which, to the best of my knowledge, is unprecedented. Putting people and values before profit, British holding companies WPP and Accenture have ceased trading in Russia. Further, practically all the large advertising agencies operating in Ukraine have offered financial support to their staff, along with access to medical advice and other practical resources. Many of these agencies have made large donations to support humanitarian efforts. Brands are taking a stance, too. In the UK, landmark department store Liberty replaced the British flag with a Ukrainian one. French luxury conglomerate LVMH temporarily closed its 124 stores in Russia; so did McDonald's (850 stores). Airbnb offered free, short-term housing to up to 100,000 refugees fleeing Ukraine.[17]

For years, marketers have been depicted (mostly accurately) as the guys selling cigarettes and encouraging excessive consumption. But after decades of depicting a utopian society, brands and their marketers are finally becoming more authentic, diverse, inclusive, and intentional; marketing is no longer only about selling toothpaste and cigarettes but also about making a positive contribution to society, culture, and the economy. In the words of Dr. EV-il, the James Bond-inspired, sympathetic villain who seeks redemption: *I will help save the world first, then take over the world.*

ACKNOWLEDGMENTS

I'm thankful for all of you who inspired *Assemblage* and helped make it a reality. In particular, thanks to Rohit Bhargava and the team at Ideapress Publishing, and Zoe Galland for the extensive editing.

Thanks to those who contributed to the case studies: Gabbie Bradford (Song Candy), Anthony Davey (Farrow & Ball), Kirby Ferguson (copy/transform/combine), and Thibault Lavergne (Wine Story).

I'm also thankful for those who inspire me and make me a better person: Derrick Daye, for his guidance and inspiration; Géraldine Michel, for inspiring the title of this book; Victoria Sakal, for being a sounding board; and Heather Marie Waymouth, for all the flashcards.

Thanks to the entire team at Ipsos, for the abundance of knowledge and ideas and the ongoing support.

And, of course, I thank my family for their support and patience: Jean and Jocelyne Probst; and Marietta, Théo, and Étienne Probst.

ABOUT THE AUTHOR

Emmanuel Probst is the Global Lead, Brand Thought Leadership at Ipsos, adjunct professor at the University of California at Los Angeles, and the author of *Wall Street Journal* and *USA Today*'s best seller *Brand Hacks*.

Emmanuel's background combines market research and brand strategy experience with strong academic achievements.

At Ipsos, Emmanuel supports numerous Fortune 500 companies by providing them with a full understanding of their customer's journey. His clients span a wide range of industries, including technology, consumer packaged goods, retail, financial services, and advertising agencies.

Emmanuel also teaches consumer market research at UCLA and writes about consumer psychology for numerous publications.

He holds an MBA in marketing from the University of Hull and a doctorate in consumer psychology from the University of Nottingham Trent.

ENDNOTES

Introduction

1. Millard, A., 2018. *Equipping James Bond*. Baltimore: Johns Hopkins University Press..

2. Millard, A., 2018. *Equipping James Bond*. Baltimore: Johns Hopkins University Press.

3. DeLanda, Manuel, 2016. *Assemblage Theory*. Edinburgh: Edinburgh University Press.

4. Schwartz, B., 2004. *The Paradox of Choice: Why More Is Less*. New York: Ecco.

5. Anderson, C., 2014. *The Long Tail*. New York: Hyperion, p. 23.

6. Spotify, 2022. *Spotify—About Spotify*. [online] Available at: <https://newsroom.spotify.com/company-info/> [Accessed 30 April 2022].

7. Spotify, 2022. *Spotify—About Spotify*. [online] Available at: <https://newsroom.spotify.com/company-info/> [Accessed 11 March 2022].

8. BBC News, 2018. *Social Media Apps Are 'Deliberately' Addictive to Users*. [online] Available at: <https://www.bbc.com/news/technology-44640959> [Accessed 11 March 2022].

9. Meaningful-brands.com, 2021. *Meaningful Brands Powered by Havas*. [online] Available at: <https://www.meaningful-brands.com/?utm_source=morning_brew> [Accessed 11 March 2022].

Chapter 1

1. Vander Veen, Steve, 1994. "The Consumption of Heroes and the Hero Hierarchy of Effects," in Chris T. Allen and Deborah Roedder John (eds.), *NA—Advances in Consumer Research*, vol. 21. Provo, UT: Association for Consumer Research, pp. 332–336.

2. Miller, D., 2017. *Building a StoryBrand*. Nashville: HarperCollins Leadership.

3. US Census Bureau, 2020. *2020 Census Statistics Highlight Population Changes and Nation's Diversity*. [online] Available at: <https://content.govdelivery.com/accounts/USCENSUS/bulletins/2ec494c> [Accessed 15 March 2022].

4. Deloitte Insights, 2022. *Authentically Inclusive Marketing*. [online] Available at: <https://www2.deloitte.com/us/en/insights/topics/marketing-and-sales-operations/global-marketing-trends/2022/diversity-and-inclusion-in-marketing.html> [Accessed 7 March 2022].

5. Lombardo, C., 2021. *Dove Shows the Girls Behind Manipulated Selfies*. [online] Strategy. Available at: <https://strategyonline.ca/2021/04/21/dove-shows-the-young-people-behind-manipulated-selfies/?utm_source=DSMN8&utm_medium=LinkedIn> [Accessed 15 March 2022].

6. Lombardo, C., 2021. *Dove Shows the Girls Behind Manipulated Selfies*. [online] Strategy. Available at: <https://strategyonline.ca/2021/04/21/dove-shows-the-young-people-behind-manipulated-selfies/?utm_source=DSMN8&utm_medium=LinkedIn> [Accessed 15 March 2022].

7. Strange, A., 2013. *Garage Where Steve Jobs Started Apple Designated as Historic Site*. [online] Mashable. Available at: <https://mashable.com/archive/steve-jobs-apple-garage-landmark> [Accessed 30 April 2022].

8. Lisy, B., 2014. *Bloomberg—Are You a Robot?* [online] Bloomberg.com. Available at: <https://www.bloomberg.com/news/articles/2014-12-04/apple-steve-wozniak-on-the-early-years-with-steve-jobs> [Accessed 30 April 2022].

9. Krause, R. and Rucker, D., 2019. *When 'Bad' Is Good: the Magnetic Attraction of Villains*. [online] Acrwebsite.org. Available at: <https://www.acrwebsite.org/volumes/2552209/volumes/v47/NA-47> [Accessed 30 April 2022].

10. Association for Psychological Science, 2020. *From Voldemort to Vader, Fictional Villains May Draw Us to Darker Versions of Ourselves: Science Says That's Okay*. [online] ScienceDaily. Available at: <https://www.sciencedaily.com/releases/2020/04/200422214031.htm> [Accessed 15 March 2022].

11. Association for Psychological Science, 2020. *From Voldemort to Vader, Fictional Villains May Draw Us to Darker Versions of Ourselves: Science Says That's Okay*. [online] ScienceDaily. Available at: <https://www.sciencedaily.com/releases/2020/04/200422214031.htm> [Accessed 15 March 2022].

12. Barnes, B., 2015. *A Family Team Looks for James Bond's Next Assignment (Published 2015).* [online] NYtimes.com. Available at: <https://www.nytimes.com/2015/11/08/business/media/a-family-team-looks-for-james-bonds-next-assignment.html> [Accessed 30 April 2022].

13. Mehta, P., 2018. *My Favourite Ad Campaign of All Time: Apple's "Here's to the Crazy Ones" from 1997.* [online] Mumbrella Asia. Available at: <https://www.mumbrella. asia/2018/07/my-favourite-ad-campaign-of-all-time-apples-heres-to-the-crazy-ones-from-1997 [Accessed 30 April 2022].

14. Harvey, J., 2019. *People Trashed That Peloton Ad So Much That Its Stock Fell Almost 10%.* [online] HuffPost UK. Available at: <https://www.huffpost.com/entry/peleton-holiday-ad-bike-stock_n_5de72b19e4b0d50f32aae376?ncid=APPLENEWS00001> [Accessed 30 April 2022].

15. Foer, F., 2019. *Jeff Bezos's Master Plan.* [online] The Atlantic. Available at: <https://www.theatlantic.com/magazine/archive/2019/11/what-jeff-bezos-wants/598363/> [Accessed 30 April 2022].

16. Foer, F., 2019. *Jeff Bezos's Master Plan.* [online] The Atlantic. Available at: <https://www.theatlantic.com/magazine/archive/2019/11/what-jeff-bezos-wants/598363/> [Accessed 30 April 2022].

17. Leamer, L., 2013. *Fantastic: The Life of Arnold Schwarzenegger.* New York: St. Martin's Press.

18. Davies, R., 2020. *The Rise and Fall of the Hummer, America's Most Needlessly Masculine Vehicle.* [online] Vox. Available at: <https://www.vox.com/the-goods/2020/1/2/20992114/hummer-masculinity-america-humvee-schwarzenegger> [Accessed 30 April 2022].

Chapter 2

1. CDC, 2022. *What Were the Trends in Antidepressant Use from 2009–2010 through 2017–2018?* [online] Available at: <https://www.cdc.gov/nchs/products/databriefs/db377.htm#:~:text=Overall percent2C percent20during percent20the percent20decade percent20between,from percent207.1 percent25 percent20to percent208.7 percent25)> [Accessed 30 April 2022].

2. Richter, F., 2022. *Infographic: Pandemic Causes Spike in Anxiety & Depression.* [online] Statista Infographics. Available at: <https://www.statista.com/chart/21878/impact-of-coronavirus-pandemic-on-mental-health/> [Accessed 30 April 2022].

3. Luminate, 2022. *MRC Data's 2021 U.S. Year-End Report.* [online] MRCdatareports.com. Available at: <https://mrcdatareports.com/mrc-data-2021-u-s-year-end-report/?utm_source=Triggermail&utm_medium=email&utm_campaign=M percent26A percent20Briefing percent20April percent206&utm_ter-

m=Marketing percent20 percent26 20Advertising%20Briefing> [Accessed 30 April 2022].

4. Ptacin, M., 2020. *Could Doomsday Bunkers Become the New Normal?* [online] NY-times.com. Available at: <https://www.nytimes.com/2020/06/26/realestate/could-doomsday-bunkers-become-the-new-normal.html> [Accessed 30 April 2022].

5. Resnick, B., 2019. *22 Percent of Millennials Say They Have "No Friends."* [online] Vox. Available at: <https://www.vox.com/science-and-health/2019/8/1/20750047/millennials-poll-loneliness> [Accessed 30 April 2022].

6. Thomas, N. J. T., 2004. "Imagination." Dictionary of Philosophy of Mind. Chris Eliasmith, ed. Available at: <http://philosophy.uwaterloo.ca/MindDict/imagination.html>.

7. Cvetkovska, L., 2022. *27 Tattoo Statistics to Intrigue, Impress & Even Encourage.* [online] Modern Gentlemen. Available at: <https://moderngentlemen.net/tattoo-statistics/#:~:text=The%20number%20of%20Americans%20with,one%20tattoo%20was%20just%2021%25.> [Accessed 30 April 2022].

8. Aside from the countless studies that have been conducted on why people get tattooed and then regret it, I like entertainer's Shannon Tanner the best: "Tattoos are a permanent reminder of a temporary feeling."

9. Allied Market Research, 2022. *Cryotherapy Market Size & Industry Forecast 2030.* [online] Allied Market Research. Available at: <https://www.alliedmarketresearch.com/cryotherapy-market-A11930#:~:text=The%20global%20cryotherapy%20market%20was,or%20lesions%2C%20and%20sports%20injuries.> [Accessed 30 April 2022].

10. Tough Mudder, 2022. *Obstacles in a Tough Mudder Mud Run | Tough Mudder USA.* [online] Tough Mudder. Available at: <https://toughmudder.com/obstacles/> [Accessed 30 April 2022].

11. Ehrenberg, A., 2009. *The Weariness of the Self: Diagnosing the History of Depression in the Contemporary Age.* Montreal: McGill-Queen's University Press.

12. Cova, V., and Cova, B., 2019. "Pain, Suffering and the Consumption of Spirituality: A Toe Story." *Journal of Marketing Management* 35(5–6), 565–585.

13. Scott, R., Cayla, J., and Cova, B., 2017. "Selling Pain to the Saturated Self." *Journal of Consumer Research* 44(1), 22–43.

14. McCracken, G., 1988. *Culture and Consumption: New Approaches to the Symbolic Character of Consumer Goods and Activities.* Bloomington: Indiana University Press.

15. Doley, R., 2022. *Sensory Branding.* [online] Neuromarketing. Available at: <https://www.neurosciencemarketing.com/blog/articles/sensory-branding.htm> [Accessed 30 April 2022].

16. Accenture, 2022. *Accenture Fjord Trends 2022.* [online] Accenture.com. Available at: <https://www.accenture.com/_acnmedia/PDF-169/Accenture-Fjord-Trends-2022-Full-Report.pdf#zoom=40> [Accessed 30 April 2022].

17. Farmer, N., Touchton-Leonard, K., and Ross, A., 2017. "Psychosocial Benefits of Cooking Interventions: A Systematic Review." *Health Education & Behavior* 45(2), 167–180.

18. Hirsh, S., 2016. *Ugg and Teva's New Mashup 'Sandals' Are Confusingly Impractical.* [online] Mashable. Available at: <https://mashable.com/article/ugg-teva-hybrid-ugly-shoes> [Accessed 30 April 2022].

19. Communication Arts, 2021. *November/December 2021 | Communication Arts.* [online] Communication Arts. Available at: <https://www.commarts.com/magazine/2021-advertising> [Accessed 30 April 2022].

Chapter 3

1. Prensky, M., 2001. *Digital Natives, Digital Immigrants.* [online] Marcprensky.com. Available at: <https://www.marcprensky.com/writing/Prensky%20-%20Digital%20Natives,%20Digital%20Immigrants%20-%20Part1.pdf> [Accessed 30 April 2022].

2. Fonseca, B., 2008. *Shuttle Columbia's Hard Drive Data Recovered from Crash Site.* [online] Computerworld. Available at: <https://www.computerworld.com/article/2535754/shuttle-columbia-s-hard-drive-data-recovered-from-crash-site.html> [Accessed 30 April 2022].

3. Baraniuk, C., 2016. *How to Destroy Your Digital History.* [online] BBC.com. Available at: <https://www.bbc.com/future/article/20160701-how-to-destroy-your-digital-history> [Accessed 30 April 2022].

4. Chatfield, T., 2017. *The Trouble with Big Data? It's Called the "Recency Bias."* [online] BBC.com. Available at: <https://www.bbc.com/future/article/20160605-the-trouble-with-big-data-its-called-the-recency-bias> [Accessed 30 April 2022].

5. Harford, T., 2014. *An Astonishing Record—of Complete Failure.* [online] FT.com. Available at: <https://www.ft.com/content/70a2a978-adac-11e7-8076-0a4bdda92ca2> [Accessed 30 April 2022].

6. Van Dijck, J., 2008. "Digital Photography: Communication, Identity, Memory." *Visual Communication* 7(1), 57–76.

7. Yong, E., 2013. *When Memories Are Remembered, They Can Be Rewritten.* [online] Science. Available at: <https://www.nationalgeographic.com/science/article/when-memories-are-remembered-they-can-be-rewritten> [Accessed 30 April 2022].

8. Resnick, B., 2018. *What Smartphone Photography Is Doing to Our Memories.* [online] Vox. Available at: <https://www.vox.com/science-and-health/2018/3/28/17054848/

smartphones-photos-memory-research-psychology-attention> [Accessed 30 April 2022].

9. Sparrow, B., 2011. *Google Effects on Memory: Cognitive Consequences of Having Information at Our Fingertips.* [online] Science. Available at: <https://www.science.org/doi/full/10.1126/science.1207745> [Accessed 27 July 2022].

10. Diehl, K., Barasch, A., and Zauberman, G. 2016. *How Taking Photos Increases Enjoyment of Experiences.* [online] Available at: <https://www.apa.org/pubs/journals/releases/psp-pspa0000055.pdf> [Accessed 27 July 2022].

11. Resnick, B., 2018. *What Smartphone Photography Is Doing to Our Memories.* [online] Vox. Available at: <https://www.vox.com/science-and-health/2018/3/28/17054848/smartphones-photos-memory-research-psychology-attention> [Accessed 30 April 2022].

12. Mantonakis, A., Whittlesea, B. W. W., and Yoon, C., 2008. "Consumer Memory, Fluency, and Familiarity." In Haugtvedt, Herr, and Kardes (eds.), *The Handbook of Consumer Psychology*, pp. 77–102. Mahwah, NJ: Lawrence Erlbaum Associates.

13. Cowan, N., 2000. "The Magical Number 4 in Short-Term Memory: A Reconsideration of Mental Storage Capacity." *Behavioural and Brain Sciences* 24, 87–125.

14. Miller, G., 1956. "The Magical Number Seven, Plus or Minus Two: Some Limits on Our Capacity for Processing Information." *Psychological Review* 63, 81–97.

15. Tulving, E., 1972. "Episodic and Semantic Memory." In E. Tulving and W. Donaldson (eds.), *Organization of Memory*, pp. 382–402). New York: Academic Press.

16. Mantonakis, A., Whittlesea, B. W. W., and Yoon, C., 2008. "Consumer Memory, Fluency, and Familiarity." In Haugtvedt, Herr, and Kardes (eds.), *The Handbook of Consumer Psychology*, pp. 77–102. Mahwah, NJ: Lawrence Erlbaum Associates.

17. Ratnayake, N., Broderick, A. J., and Mitchell, R. L. C., 2010. "A Neurocognitive Approach to Brand Memory." *Journal of Marketing Management* 26, 1295–1318.

18. Sharp, B., 2010. *How Brands Grow: What Marketers Don't Know.* South Melbourne, Victoria, Australia: Oxford University Press.

19. Kofoed, J., and Larsen, M. C., 2016. "A Snap of Intimacy: Photo-Sharing Practices among Young People on Social Media." *First Monday* 21(11).

20. Kotfila, C., 2014. "This Message Will Self Destruct: The Growing Role of Obscurity and Self Destructing Data in Digital Communication." *Bulletin of the Association for Information Science and Technology* 40(2), 12–16.

21. Kivetz, R., and He, D., 2017. *Being in the Moment: The Effect of Ephemeral Communication in Social Media.* [online] MSI.org. Available at: <https://www.msi.org/wp-content/uploads/2020/06/MSI_Report_17-112-1.pdf> [Accessed 30 April 2022].

22. Bishop, S., Lau, M., Shapiro, S., Carlson, L., Anderson, N., Carmody, J., Segal, Z., Abbey, S., Speca, M., Velting, D., and Devins, G., 2004. "Mindfulness: A Proposed Operational Definition." *Clinical Psychology: Science and Practice* 11(3), 230–241.

23. Vanderslice, P., 2020. *Review: Netflix's "The Social Dilemma" Is a Great Conversation Starter, but Not Enough to Create Change.* [online] Available at: <https://sundial.csun.edu/161195/arts-entertainment/review-netflixs-the-social-dilemma-is-a-great-conversation-starter-but-not-enough-to-create-change/> [Accessed 30 April 2022].

24. Most of us had not heard the term "metaverse" until October 2021, when Mark Zuckerberg positioned it as the future of the internet and social media and renamed Facebook's parent company "Meta." Mark Zuckerberg was not a genius for predicting and naming the future. Facebook paid a Sioux Falls, South Dakota, community bank $60 million for the name "Meta." What's more, in 1992, American writer Neal Stephenson published *Snow Crash*, a sci-fi novel that tells the story of Hiro Protagonist, a hacker and pizza delivery driver who goes back and forth between a dystopian Los Angeles and a virtual world called The Metaverse.

25. Casper, J., 2022. *Alter Ego: Avatars and their Creators—Photographs by Robbie Cooper | LensCulture.* [online] LensCulture. Available at: <https://www.lensculture.com/articles/robbie-cooper-alter-ego-avatars-and-their-creators> [Accessed 30 April 2022].

26. Emarketer, 2021. *Mobile AR Advertising Revenues Worldwide, 2020–2025.* [online] Available at: <https://chart-na1.emarketer.com/248314/mobile-ar-advertising-revenues-worldwide-2020-2025-billions> [Accessed 30 April 2022].

27. Hew-Low, K., 2022. *My Ancestral Home, the Mall.* [online] The Drift. <https://www.thedriftmag.com/my-ancestral-home-the-mall/> [Accessed 30 April 2022].

Chapter 4

1. Beilock, S., 2020. *Why Young Americans Are Lonely.* [online] Scientific American. Available at: <https://www.scientificamerican.com/article/why-young-americans-are-lonely/#:~:text=And%20a%20survey%20released%20in,on%20cultivating%20and%20maintaining%20relationships.> [Accessed 1 May 2022].

2. Clark, P., 2021. *Zillow Shuts Home-Flipping Business after Racking Up Losses.* [online] Bloomberg.com. Available at: <https://www.bloomberg.com/news/articles/2021-11-02/zillow-shuts-down-home-flipping-business-after-racking-up-losses> [Accessed 1 May 2022].

3. Perez, S., 2021. TikTok Just Gave Itself Permission to Collect Biometric Data on US Users, Including "Faceprints and Voiceprints." [online] TechCrunch. Available at: <https://techcrunch.com/2021/06/03/tiktok-just-gave-itself-permission-to-collect-biometric-data-on-u-s-users-including-faceprints-and-voiceprints/?guccounter=1> [Accessed 1 May 2022].

4. Probst, E., 2021. *Public More Open to Tech Companies Sharing Their Data —But There's a Limit.* [online] Ipsos.com. Available at: <https://www.ipsos.com/en-us/knowledge/

media-brand-communication/Public-More-Open-to-Tech-Companies-Sharing-their-Data-But-There-is-a-Limit> [Accessed 1 May 2022].

5. Gilchrist, K., 2017. *Chatbots Expected to Cut Business Costs by $8 Billion by 2022.* [online] Available at: <https://www.cnbc.com/2017/05/09/chatbots-expected-to-cut-business-costs-by-8-billion-by-2022.html> [Accessed 1 May 2022].

6. Morgan, B., 2020. *Customer Journeys Are Becoming Increasingly Complex.* [online] Forbes. Available at: <https://www.forbes.com/sites/blakemorgan/2020/08/31/customer-journeys-are-becoming-increasingly-complex/?sh=596de68339b4> [Accessed 1 May 2022].

7. Ipsos study for Unstereotype Alliance, 2021.

8. Ipsos social value research, 2021.

9. Bowler, H., 2022. *Ogilvy Will No Longer Work with Influencers Who Edit Their Bodies or Faces for Ads.* [online] The Drum. Available at: <https://www.thedrum.com/news/2022/04/07/ogilvy-will-no-longer-work-with-influencers-who-edit-their-bodies-or-faces-ads> [Accessed 1 May 2022].

10. Adweek, 2021. *I'm With the Brand | Omsom Is on a Mission to Reclaim Asian Flavors in Grocery Stores.* [online] YouTube.com. Available at: <https://www.youtube.com/watch?v=TqsCthIHca8> [Accessed 1 May 2022].

11. Adweek, 2021. *I'm With the Brand | Omsom Is on a Mission to Reclaim Asian Flavors in Grocery Stores.* [online] YouTube.com. Available at: <https://www.youtube.com/watch?v=TqsCthIHca8> [Accessed 1 May 2022].

12. Design Driven NYC, 2021. *Cutting through the Noise: How to Build a Brand with Cultural Resonance.* [online] Youtube.com. Available at: <https://www.youtube.com/watch?v=nPmB1pNixRI> [Accessed 1 May 2022].

13. Jenkins, P., and Vieira, B., 2020. *Europe's Digital Migration During COVID-19: Getting Past the Broad Trends and Averages.* [online] Available at: <https://www.mckinsey.com/business-functions/mckinsey-digital/our-insights/europes-digital-migration-during-covid-19-getting-past-the-broad-trends-and-averages> [Accessed 1 May 2022].

14. Daae, L., 2020. *Go Digital Go Green.* [online] Capgemini Worldwide. Available at: <https://www.capgemini.com/2020/05/go-digital-go-green/> [Accessed 1 May 2022].

15. Mehalchin, M., 2020. *A Brief History of DTC.* [online] Concentrix Catalyst. Available at: <https://pkglobal.com/blog/2020/09/brief-history-dtc/> [Accessed 1 May 2022].

16. Thau, B., 2022. *How a New Wave of DTC Startups Are Tapping Big Retail to Scale Growth.* [online] https://www.uschamber.com/co. Available at: <https://www.

uschamber.com/co/good-company/launch-pad/dtc-startups-tap-big-retail-to-grow>
[Accessed 1 May 2022].

17. Flint, J., 2022. *Netflix to Sell "Squid Game" Goods, Other Products on Walmart Site.* [online] WSJ. Available at: <https://www.wsj.com/articles/netflix-to-sell-squid-game-goods-other-products-on-walmart-site-11633928460> [Accessed 1 May 2022].

18. Salpini, C., 2021. *These Traditional Brands Are Shifting to a DTC Model. Here's How.* [online] Retail Dive. Available at: <https://www.retaildive.com/news/these-traditional-brands-are-shifting-to-a-dtc-model-heres-how/607646/> [Accessed 1 May 2022].

19. Salpini, C., 2021. *Adidas Aims for DTC to Be 50% of Sales by 2025.* [online] Retail Dive. Available at: <https://www.retaildive.com/news/adidas-aims-for-dtc-to-be-50-of-sales-by-2025/596509/> [Accessed 1 May 2022].

20. Unglesbee, B., 2021. *Analysts Throw Cold Water on the Great DTC Pivot.* [online] Retail Dive. Available at: <https://www.retaildive.com/news/analysts-throw-cold-water-on-the-great-dtc-pivot/607209/> [Accessed 1 May 2022].

21. Sherwood., I., 2021. *Marketers Are Quitting Their Jobs—Why the Industry Should Brace for an Exodus.* [online] Ad Age. Available at: <https://adage.com/article/agency-news/marketers-are-quitting-their-jobs-what-exodus-means-industry/2346881> [Accessed 1 May 2022].

22. Paper & Packaging, 2022. *Inside Unboxing: How Boxes Deliver Psychological Payoffs.* [online] Paper & Packaging. Available at: <https://www.howlifeunfolds.com/packaging-innovation/inside-unboxing-how-boxes-deliver-psychological-payoffs> [Accessed 1 May 2022].

Chapter 5

1. Public Affairs, 2008. *The Political Brain.* [online] Available at: <https://www.publicaffairsbooks.com/titles/drew-westen/the-political-brain/9781586485993/> [Accessed 15 March 2022].

2. Supersmile, 2022. *Extra Whitening Bundles.* [online] Available at: <https://www.supersmile.com/products/extra-whitening-bundles> [Accessed 15 March 2022].

3. Grey Goose, 2019. *Grey Goose® Vodka Invites People to Treat Themselves as the Special Occasion with the Launch of Live Victoriously.* [online] PRNewswire.com. Available at: <https://www.prnewswire.com/news-releases/grey-goose-vodka-invites-people-to-treat-themselves-as-the-special-occasion-with-the-launch-of-live-victoriously-300833901.html#:~:text=%22At%20its%20core%2C%20Live%20Victoriously,to%20create%20a%20lifelong%20memory.> [Accessed 15 March 2022].

4. Fleming, M., 2019. *Diageo Wants to Make Lower Calorie Alcohol 'Interesting' with Premium Flavoured Spirits.* [online] Marketingweek.com. Available at: <https://www.market-

ingweek.com/diageo-ketel-one-premium-flavoured-vodka/> [Accessed 15 March 2022].

5. Ritson, M., 2022. *Brand Might Slyly Alter Human Truth: How Brand Image Changes Perceptions of Reality*. [online] Marketingweek.com. Available at: <https://www.marketingweek.com/mark-ritson-brand-image-perceptions-reality/> [Accessed 15 March 2022].

6. Topolinski, S., 2009. *A Fluency-Affect Intuition Model*. Würzburg: Universität Würzburg.

7. Roller, C., 2011. *How Cognitive Fluency Affects Decision Making: UXmatters*. [online] Uxmatters.com. Available at: <https://www.uxmatters.com/mt/archives/2011/07/how-cognitive-fluency-affects-decision-making.php> [Accessed 15 March 2022].

8. Rajagopal, P., and Montgomery, N., 2011. "I Imagine, I Experience, I Like: The False Experience Effect." *Journal of Consumer Research* 38(3), 578-594.

9. Rajagopal, P., and Montgomery, N., 2011. "I Imagine, I Experience, I Like: The False Experience Effect." *Journal of Consumer Research* 38(3), 578-594.

10. YouTube.com, 2017. *Kellyanne Conway: Press Secretary Sean Spicer Gave 'Alternative Facts' | Meet The Press | NBC News*. [online] Available at: <https://www.youtube.com/watch?v=VSrEEDQgFc8> [Accessed 30 April 2022].

11. Reynolds, E., 2018. *Why Our Brains Love Fake News—and How We Can Resist It*. [online] NYU.edu. Available at: <https://www.nyu.edu/about/news-publications/news/2018/june/jay-van-bavel-on-fake-news.html> [Accessed 15 March 2022].

12. Festinger, L., Riecken, H. W., and Schachter, S., 1964. *When Prophecy Fails: A Social and Psychological Study of a Modern Group That Predicted the Destruction of the World*. New York: Harper & Row.

13. McCarthy, T., and Strauss, D., 2020. *How Trump's* Apprentice *Earnings Helped Rescue His Failing Empire*. [online] The Guardian. Available at: <https://www.theguardian.com/us-news/2020/sep/29/trump-tax-returns-the-apprentice-empire> [Accessed 15 March 2022].

14. Trump's tax filings reveal that he earned $427 million from the fourteen seasons of *The Apprentice* and associated endorsement and licensing deals. He used the funds to cover the losses of his real estate and hospitality "empire." These same filings reveal that had Trump not played the role of a successful billionaire on TV, his actual earnings would have been flat from 2000 to 2018, leaving him unable to repay the debts incurred from his casino projects.

15. Nast, C., 2020. *Trump Wrote Off More Money for Hairstyling Than Most Americans Make in a Year*. [online] Allure. Available at: <https://www.allure.com/story/trump-hair-tax-return-deduction> [Accessed 11 March 2022].

16. Jehner, K., 2021. *Core Trump Asset—His Brand—Transformed as He Returns to Business.* [online] News.bloomberglaw.com. Available at: <https://news.bloomberglaw.com/ip-law/core-trump-asset-his-brand-transformed-as-he-returns-to-business> [Accessed 15 March 2022].

17. MBA Today, 2022. *Methodology of MBA Rankings: How Do Media Rank Schools?* [online] Available at: <https://www.mba.today/guide/methodology-of-mba-rankings> [Accessed 15 March 2022].

18. Levy, P., 2016. *Benoît Violier: Chef Whose Restaurant Was Named Best in the World.* [online] The Independent. Available at: <https://www.independent.co.uk/news/obituaries/benoit-violier-chef-whose-perfectionist-rigour-led-to-his-restaurant-in-lausanne-being-recently-named-as-the-best-in-the-world-a6857006.html> [Accessed 15 March 2022].

19. Kelly, D., 2018. *The Untold Truth of the Michelin Guide.* [online] Mashed.com. Available at: <https://www.mashed.com/126793/the-untold-truth-of-the-michelin-guide/#:~:text=He20says%20there%20were%20only,they're%20reviewing%20each%20year.> [Accessed 15 March 2022].

20. Holbrook, Morris B., and Zirlin, Robert B., 1985. "Artistic Creation, Artworks, and Aesthetic Appreciation: Some Philosophical Contributions to Nonprofit Marketing." In Russell W. Belk (ed.), *Advances in Nonprofit Marketing,* vol. 1, pp. 1–54. Greenwich, CT: JAI Press.

21. Forty, A., 2000. *Objects of Desire.* London: Thames and Hudson.

22. Carroll, N., 2001. *Beyond Aesthetics: Philosophical Essays.* Cambridge: Cambridge University Press.

23. Sontag, S., 2014. *On Photography.* New York: Picador.

24. Prevos, P., 2011. *The Magic of Marketing.* [online] Lucidmanager.org. Available at: <https://lucidmanager.org/marketing/marketing-magic/> [Accessed 15 March 2022].

25. Miller, M., 2022. *How Long Does It Take for a Sleight of Hand Magician to Learn the Craft?* [online] Quora. Available at: <https://www.quora.com/How-long-does-it-take-for-a-sleight-of-hand-magician-to-learn-the-craft> [Accessed 15 March 2022].

Chapter 6

1. Yuan, Y., and Constine, J., 2022. *What is the Creator Economy?* [online] SignalFire. Available at: <https://signalfire.com/blog/creator-economy/> [Accessed 1 May 2022].

2. NYtimes.com, 2021. *Opinion | Is the Rise of the Substack Economy Bad for Democracy?* [online] Available at: <https://www.nytimes.com/2021/07/08/opinion/substack-facebook-bulletin-journalism.html> [Accessed 11 March 2022].

3.   Ingham, T., 2020. *Spotify Dreams of Artists Making a Living. It Probably Won't Come True.* [online] Rolling Stone. Available at: <https://www.rollingstone.com/pro/features/spotify-million-artists-royalties-1038408/> [Accessed 11 March 2022].

4.   Hautman, N., 2022. *Scooter Addresses Taylor's New Albums, Says Weaponizing Fans Is 'Dangerous'.* [online] Us Weekly. Available at: <https://www.usmagazine.com/celebrity-news/pictures/taylor-swift-big-machine-records-fallout-everything-we-know/back-in-the-studio-2/> [Accessed 1 May 2022].

5.   Steele, A., 2021. *Taylor Swift's Rerecording of 'Red' Is Reshaping the Music Industry.* [online] WSJ. Available at: <https://www.wsj.com/story/taylor-swifts-rerecording-of-red-is-reshaping-the-music-industry-ef6c7d66> [Accessed 1 May 2022].

6.   Liederman, E., 2022. Agency Highsnobiety Just Put TikTok's Favorite Trainspotter in the Conductor's Seat for Gucci. [online] Adweek.com. Available at: <https://www.adweek.com/agencies/agency-highsnobiety-just-put-tiktoks-favorite-trainspotter-in-the-conductors-seat-for-gucci/> [Accessed 1 May 2022].

7.   Highsnobiety, 2022. *Birdwatching with Gucci, The North Face and Flock Together.* [online] Highsnobiety. Available at: <https://www.highsnobiety.com/p/gucci-the-north-face-flock-together/> [Accessed 1 May 2022].

8.   Sato, M., 2022. *Reselling Gig Work Is TikTok's Newest Side Hustle.* [online] The Verge. Available at: <https://www.theverge.com/22905356/gig-work-drop-shipping-fiverr-tiktok> [Accessed 1 May 2022].

9.   Forstadt, A., 2022. *Trending Etsy Business Ideas to Consider.* [online] https://www.uschamber.com/co. Available at: <https://www.uschamber.com/co/start/business-ideas/trending-etsy-business-ideas> [Accessed 1 May 2022].

10. PBS, 2022. *Triumph of the Nerds: The Transcripts, Part III.* [online] PBS.org. Available at: <http://www.pbs.org/nerds/part3.html> [Accessed 1 May 2022].

11. PBS, 2022. *Triumph of the Nerds: The Transcripts, Part III.* [online] PBS.org. Available at: <http://www.pbs.org/nerds/part3.html> [Accessed 1 May 2022].

12. Grant, A., 2016. *The Surprising Habits of Original Thinkers.* [online] TED.com. Available at: <https://www.ted.com/talks/adam_grant_the_surprising_habits_of_original_thinkers?language=en> [Accessed 1 May 2022].

13. Godin, S., 2008. *Tribes.* New York: Portfolio.

14. Cova, B., 1997. "Community and Consumption: Towards a Definition of the Linking Value of Products or Services," *European Journal of Marketing* 31(3/4), 297–316.

15. Cova, B., and Cova, V., 2001. "Tribal Aspects of Postmodern Consumption Research: The Case of French In-Line Roller Skaters," *Journal of Consumer Behavior* 1(1), 67–76.

16. Cova, B., and Cova, V., 2002. "Tribal Marketing: The Tribalisation of Society and Its Impact on the Conduct of Marketing," *European Journal of Marketing* 36(5/6), 595–620.

17. Shank, I., 2022. *Four Iconic Quotes Artists Never Actually Said.* [online] Artsy. Available at: <https://www.artsy.net/article/artsy-editorial-four-iconic-quotes-artists> [Accessed 1 May 2022].

Chapter 7

1. Lorenz, T., Browning, K., and Frenkel, S., 2020. *TikTok Teens and K-Pop Stans Say They Sank Trump Rally.* [online] NYtimes.com. Available at: <https://www.nytimes.com/2020/06/21/style/tiktok-trump-rally-tulsa.html> [Accessed 15 March 2022].

2. Credit.com, 2022. *Explained: The Adrenaline-Driven Rise to GameStop Stock.* [online] Available at: <https://www.credit.com/blog/gamestop-stock-explained/> [Accessed 15 March 2022].

3. Jones, O., 2022. *Woke-Washing: How Brands Are Cashing in on the Culture Wars.* [online] The Guardian. Available at: <https://www.theguardian.com/media/2019/may/23/woke-washing-brands-cashing-in-on-culture-wars-owen-jones> [Accessed 15 March 2022].

4. Companiesmarketcap.com, 2022. *Marks & Spencer (MAKSF)—Revenue.* [online] Available at: <https://companiesmarketcap.com/marks-and-spencer/revenue/> [Accessed 15 March 2022].

5. Young, S., 2019. *A UK Supermarket Released an 'LGBT' Sandwich for Charity, and People Don't Know How They Feel about It.* [online] Business Insider. Available at: <https://www.businessinsider.com/marks-and-spencer-lgbt-sandwich-receives-mixed-reactions-2019-5> [Accessed 15 March 2022].

6. Busby, M., and Snaith, E., 2018. *Stonewall and Primark Criticised for Pride T-shirts Made in Turkey.* [online] The Guardian. Available at: <https://www.theguardian.com/world/2018/aug/02/stonewall-and-primark-criticised-pride-t-shirts-made-in-turkey-lgbt-rights> [Accessed 15 March 2022].

7. Abad-Santos, A., 2018. *Nike's Colin Kaepernick Ad Sparked a Boycott— and Earned $6 Billion for Nike.* [online] Vox. Available at: <https://www.vox.com/2018/9/24/17895704/nike-colin-kaepernick-boycott-6-billion> [Accessed 15 March 2022].

8. Martinez, G., 2018. *Nike Sales Increase 31% after Kaepernick Ad Despite Backlash.* [online] Time. Available at: <https://time.com/5390884/nike-sales-go-up-kaepernick-ad/> [Accessed 15 March 2022].

9. Carroll, B., and Ahuvia, A., 2006. "Some Antecedents and Outcomes of Brand Love," *Marketing Letters*, 17(2), 79–89.

10. Belk, R. W., 1988. "Possessions and the Extended Self," *Journal of Consumer Research* 15(2), 139–168.

11. Grandviewresearch.com, 2019. *Global Cake Mixes Market Size, Share | Industry Report, 2019–2025.* [online] Available at: <https://www.grandviewresearch.com/industry-analysis/cake-mixes-market> [Accessed 15 March 2022].

12. Norton, M., Mochon, D., and Ariely, D., 2011. "The 'IKEA Effect': When Labor Leads to Love," *SSRN Electronic Journal.*

13. Sinclair, A., 2021. *Is Harley-Davidson Heading for a Crash?.* [online] Speedwaydigest. com. Available at: <https://www.speedwaydigest.com/index.php/news/racing-news/61552-is-harley-davidson-heading-for-a-crash> [Accessed 15 March 2022].

14. Walker, M., 2021. *U.S. Newsroom Employment Has Fallen 26% since 2008.* [online] Pew Research Center. Available at: <https://www.pewresearch.org/fact-tank/2021/07/13/u-s-newsroom-employment-has-fallen-26-since-2008/> [Accessed 15 March 2022].

15. Netimperative, 2019. *Cannes Lions Winner: Carrefour 'Black Supermarket' Wins Creative Effectiveness—Netimperative.* [online] Available at: <https://www.netimperative. com/2019/06/25/cannes-lions-winner-carrefour-black-supermarket-wins-creative-effectiveness> [Accessed 15 March 2022].

16. Medium, 2019. *Benetton Invented Modern Marketing.* [online] Available at: <https:// medium.com/swlh/benetton-invented-modern-marketing-c35a04299ecc> [Accessed 15 March 2022].

17. Medium, 2019. *Benetton Invented Modern Marketing.* [online] Available at: <https:// medium.com/swlh/benetton-invented-modern-marketing-c35a04299ecc> [Accessed 15 March 2022].

18. Povoledo, E., 2020. *Benetton Severs Ties with Oliviero Toscani.* [online] nytimes.com. Available at: <https://www.nytimes.com/2020/02/06/world/europe/benetton-oliviero-toscani.html> [Accessed 15 March 2022].

Chapter 8

1. Bodley, D., and Liedtke, A., 2021. *Even Big Brands Need a Direct-to-Consumer Strategy.* [online] BCG Global. Available at: <https://www.bcg.com/publications/2021/direct-to-consumer-strategy-business-benefits> [Accessed 1 May 2022].

2. The Challenger Project, 2021. *Bookshop—For Challenging Amazon.* [online] The Challenger Project | The Home of Challenger Brands. Available at: <https:// thechallengerproject.com/blog/challenger-brands-to-watch-2021-bookshop> [Accessed 1 May 2022].

3. Betinelli, M., 2022. *Slowear18—The Fashion Store Turns into a Mixology Bar at Night.* [online] TRENDLAND | Online Trend News. Available at: <https://trendland. com/slowear18-fashion-store-bar-at-night/> [Accessed 1 May 2022].

4. Fona, 2020. *TREND INSIGHT: Premiumization.* [online] Fona.com. Available at: <http://www.fona.com/wp-content/uploads/2020/04/0520-FONA-Premiumization-report-2.pdf> [Accessed 1 May 2022].

5. Kuffel, J., 2021. *Premiumization: How Smart Brands Become Category Leaders.* [online] Pricefx. Available at: <https://www.pricefx.com/learning-center/premiumization-how-smart-brands-become-category-leaders/> [Accessed 1 May 2022].

6. Conklin, A., 2021. *How Many Movies Are on Netflix?* [online] Fox Business. Available at: <https://www.foxbusiness.com/technology/how-many-movies-on-netflix> [Accessed 1 May 2022].

7. Kehoe, B., 2016. *The Best Place to Hide a Dead Body—Leverage Marketing.* [online] Leverage Marketing. Available at: <https://www.theleverageway.com/blog/real-deal-with-bob-kehoe-best-place-to-hide-a-dead-body/#:~:text=But%20the%20best%20hiding%20place,a%20slender%208.5%25%20of%20clicks.> [Accessed 1 May 2022].

8. Politt, C., 2014. *The Best Place to Hide a Dead Body Is Page Two of Google.* [online] HuffPost. Available at: <https://www.huffpost.com/entry/the-best-place-to-hide-a-_b_5168714> [Accessed 1 May 2022].

Chapter 9

1. Tradingeconomics.com, 2022. *United States Consumer Spending—2022 Data—2023 Forecast—1950–2021 Historical.* [online] Tradingeconomics.com. Available at: <https://tradingeconomics.com/united-states/consumer-spending> [Accessed 1 May 2022].

2. Lay, J., 2019. *America's Dopamine-Fueled Shopping Addiction.* [online] The Atlantic. Available at: <https://www.theatlantic.com/video/index/583372/consumerism/> [Accessed 1 May 2022].

3. Saveonenergy.com, 2022. *Land of Waste: American Landfills and Waste Production.* [online] Saveonenergy.com. Available at: <https://www.saveonenergy.com/land-of-waste/> [Accessed 1 May 2022].

4. Earth911, 2021. *20 Staggering E-Waste Facts in 2021.* [online] Earth911. Available at: <https://earth911.com/eco-tech/20-e-waste-facts/> [Accessed 1 May 2022].

5. Wicker, A., 2016. *The Earth Is Covered in the Waste of Your Old Clothes.* [online] Newsweek. Available at: <https://www.newsweek.com/2016/09/09/old-clothes-fashion-waste-crisis-494824.html> [Accessed 1 May 2022].

6. Association for Psychological Science, 2012. *Consumerism and Its Antisocial Effects Can Be Turned On—or Off.* [online] Association for Psychological Science. Available at: <https://www.psychologicalscience.org/news/releases/consumerism-and-its-antisocial-effects-can-be-turned-onor-off.html> [Accessed 1 May 2022].

7. Jayson, S., 2019. *Social Media Doesn't Stop Generation Z, Millennials from Feeling Lonely, Survey Finds.* [online] NBC News. Available at: <https://www.nbcnews.com/health/

health-news/despite-social-media-generation-z-millennials-report-feeling-lonely-n980926> [Accessed 1 May 2022].

8. Williams-Grut, O., 2017. *People Prefer Tap Water over 'Premium' £1.49 Fiji Water in a Blind Taste Test.* [online] Business Insider. Available at: <https://www.businessinsider.com/blind-taste-test-tap-water-premium-fiji-water-evian-2017-5> [Accessed 1 May 2022].

9. Ipsos, 2021. *Ipsos Global Trends.* [online] Ipsos.com. Available at: <https://www.ipsos.com/sites/default/files/ct/publication/documents/2021-10/IM_October21_v1.pdf> [Accessed 1 May 2022].

10. DS Smith, 2022. *Sustainable Packaging. Has the COVID-19 Pandemic Changed Everything?* [online] DSsmith.com. Available at: <https://www.dssmith.com/globalassets/packaging/country-sites/11_czech-republic/the-impact-of-the-covid-19-pandemic-on-sustainable-packaging-ds-smith-and-ipsos-mori-research.pdf> [Accessed 1 May 2022].

11. LVMH, 2020. *Ruinart Unveils New Eco-Designed, 100% Recyclable Packaging at Vinexpo Trade Fair.* [online] LVMH. Available at: <https://www.lvmh.com/news-documents/news/ruinart-unveils-new-eco-designed-100-recyclable-packaging-at-vinexpo-trade-fair> [Accessed 1 May 2022].

12. Yang, J., and Battocchio, A., 2020. "Effects of Transparent Brand Communication on Perceived Brand Authenticity and Consumer Responses," *Journal of Product & Brand Management* 30(8), 1176–1193.

13. Bain, M., 2017. *H&M's New Brand, Arket, Names the Factory That Made Its Clothes. But the Name Isn't Enough.* [online] Quartz. Available at: <https://qz.com/1064098/hms-new-brand-arket-is-fashiontransparency-conundrum-in-a-nutshell/> [Accessed 1 May 2022].

14. Brown, E., 2018. *9 out of 10 Consumers Will Stop Purchasing from Brands That Lack Transparency | ZDNet.* [online] ZDNet. Available at: <https://www.zdnet.com/article/9-out-of-10-consumers-will-stop-purchasing-from-brands-that-lack-transparency/> [Accessed 11 March 2022].

15. Mollah, S., and Bin Habib, W., 2022. *It Crumbles Like a Pack of Cards.* [online] The Daily Star. Available at: <https://www.thedailystar.net/news/like-a-pack-of-cards-it-crumbles> [Accessed 1 May 2022].

16. Kamleitner, Bernadette, Thürridl, Carina, and Martin, Brett, 2019. "A Cinderella Story: How Past Identity Salience Boosts Demand for Repurposed Products," *Journal of Marketing* 83, 002224291987215. 10.1177/0022242919872156.

17. Centennial Light, 2022. *Livermore's Centennial Light Bulb.* [online] Centennialbulb.org. Available at: <http://www.centennialbulb.org/index.htm> [Accessed 1 May 2022].

18. Centennial Light, 2022. *Livermore's Centennial Light Bulb.* [online] Centennialbulb.org. Available at: <http://www.centennialbulb.org/index.htm> [Accessed 1 May 2022].

Chapter 10

1. Widmaier Picasso, O., 2004. *Picasso: The Real Family Story.* New York: Prestel, p. 275.
2. Richardson, J., McCully, M., Finocchio, R., and Huisinga, D., 2007. *A Life of Picasso.* New York: Alfred A. Knopf.
3. Aam-us.com, 2022. *Museum Facts & Data.* [online] Available at: <https://www.aam-us.org/programs/about-museums/museum-facts-data/> [Accessed 15 March 2022].
4. Celeb Depositions, 2014. *Pharrell Williams: "You Were Trying to Pretend You Were Marvin Gaye?"* [online] Available at: https://www.youtube.com/watch?v=sOp17HQWc0Y [Accessed 15 March 2022].
5. Wete, B., 2012. *What Does DJ Khaled Do and Is He Good for Hip-Hop?.* [online] Complex.com. Available at: <https://www.complex.com/music/2012/08/what-does-dj-khaled-do-and-is-he-good-for-hip-hop> [Accessed 15 March 2022].
6. Rodic, D., 2019. *DJ Khaled Teaches You the Keys to Sonic Branding.* [online] Medium. Available at: <https://medium.com/@drodic/dj-khaled-teaches-you-the-to-sonic-branding-f614302d561e> [Accessed 15 March 2022].
7. Ortiz, N., 2020. *How DJ Khaled Has Made Confidence a Brand—and a Formula for Outsize Success.* [online] Adweek.com. Available at: <https://www.adweek.com/brand-marketing/how-dj-khaled-has-made-confidence-a-brand-and-a-formula-for-outsize-success/> [Accessed 15 March 2022].
8. Shaw, A., 2019. *Jeff Koons Says Computer Technology Allowed Him to Downsize His New York Studio.* [online] Theartnewspaper.com. Available at: <https://www.theartnewspaper.com/news/jeff-koons-says-computer-technology-allowed-him-to-downsize-his-new-york-studio> [Accessed 15 March 2022].
9. Horkheimer, M., and Adorno, T., 1998. *Dialectic of Enlightenment.* New York: Continuum.
10. Boucher, B., 2018. *Art-World Hookup: OkCupid Hired Artist Maurizio Cattelan to Create Its First-Ever Ad Campaign | Artnet News.* [online] Artnet News. Available at: <https://news.artnet.com/art-world/maurizio-cattelan-okcupid-ad-campaign-1185068> [Accessed 15 March 2022].
11. Eliasson, O., 2016. *Why Art Has the Power to Change the World.* [online] World Economic Forum. Available at: <https://www.weforum.org/agenda/2016/01/why-art-has-the-power-to-change-the-world/> [Accessed 15 March 2022].
12. Judkis, M., 2017. *Forget the Handmade Wreaths. Now Martha Stewart Hangs with Snoop Dogg and Makes Weed Jokes.* [online] Washington Post. Available at: <https://www.washingtonpost.com/lifestyle/food/forget-the-handmade-wreaths-now-martha-

stewart-hangs-with-snoop-dogg-and-makes-weed-jokes/2017/10/14/c901ae5c-aabe-11e7-850e-2bdd1236be5d_story.html?utm_term=.fcf6421aed68&itid=lk_in-line_manual_1> [Accessed 15 March 2022].

13. Stewart and Snoop Dogg share the experience of time behind bars. Stewart served almost five months after being found guilty on three counts in connection with her sale of ImClone Systems stock three years earlier. Snoop Dogg was arrested several times between 1989 and 1992 for possession and sale of drugs.

14. Campaignlive.com, 2022. *Snoop Dogg and Martha Stewart Light up for BIC.* [online] Available at: <https://www.campaignlive.com/article/snoop-dogg-martha-stewart-light-bic/1736759> [Accessed 15 March 2022].

15. Hammond, H., 2022. *BIC Taps Snoop Dogg, Martha Stewart for New Ad.* [online] CSP Daily News. Available at: <https://www.cspdailynews.com/tobacco/bic-taps-snoop-dogg-martha-stewart-new-ad> [Accessed 15 March 2022].

16. Jäncke, L., 2008. "Music, Memory and Emotion." *Journal of Biology* 7(6), 21.

Now, It Is Your Turn

1. Pasquarelli, A., 2021. *New Nike Spot Encourages "Giving It a Shot, Even Though Your Shot Is Garbage."* [online] Ad Age. Available at: <https://adage.com/article/cmo-strategy/new-nike-spot-encourages-giving-it-shot-even-though-your-shot-garbage/2333381> [Accessed 1 May 2022].

2. Digital Synopsis, 2022. *Why Page 2 of Google Search Results Is the Best Place to Hide a Dead Body.* [online] Digital Synopsis. Available at: <https://digitalsynopsis.com/tools/google-serp-design> [Accessed 1 May 2022].

3. Chayka, K., 2016. *How Silicon Valley Helps Spread the Same Sterile Aesthetic across the World.* [online] The Verge. Available at: <https://www.theverge.com/2016/8/3/12325104/airbnb-aesthetic-global-minimalism-startup-gentrification> [Accessed 1 May 2022].

4. Stevenson, S., 2013. *Was "We Try Harder" the Most Brilliant Ad Slogan of the 20th Century?* [online] Slate Magazine. Available at: <https://slate.com/business/2013/08/hertz-vs-avis-advertising-wars-how-an-ad-firm-made-a-virtue-out-of-second-place.html> [Accessed 1 May 2022].

5. Patterson, D., 2016. *Penn & Teller.* [online] Doug Patterson. Available at: <https://www.dougpatterson.com/xii> [Accessed 1 May 2022].

6. Automotive News Europe, 2021. *Ferrari Signals Higher Profits after Record 2021.* [online] Automotive News Europe. Available at: <https://europe.autonews.com/automakers/ferrari-signals-higher-profits-after-record-2021> [Accessed 1 May 2022].

7. Ritson, M., 2021. *John Lewis the Landlord? Welcome to Brand Extension Nirvana.* [online] Available at: <https://www.marketingweek.com/mark-ritson-john-lewis-brand-extension/> [Accessed 1 May 2022].

8. Kärcher, 2022. *Monuments of the World—Cultural Sponsorship | Kärcher International.* [online] Kaercher.com. Available at: <https://www.kaercher.com/int/inside-kaercher/company/sponsoring/cultural-sponsorship.html> [Accessed 1 May 2022].

9. Google Trends, 2022. *Kärcher.* [online] Available at: <https://trends.google.fr/trends/explore?date=today%203-m&geo=FR&q=%2Fm%2F085rqy> [Accessed 1 May 2022].

10. Roznik, S., 2016. *Funeral Home Billboards Grim Reminder to Teens.* [online] FDL Reporter. Available at: <https://www.fdlreporter.com/story/news/local/2016/03/09/funeral-home-billboards-grim-reminder-teens/81493122/> [Accessed 1 May 2022].

11. DeadHappy, 2022. *Homepage.* [online] DeadHappy. Available at: <https://deadhappy.com/> [Accessed 1 May 2022].

12. Mentalhealth.org.uk, 2021. *Mental Health Statistics: Suicide.* [online] Mental Health Foundation. Available at: <https://www.mentalhealth.org.uk/statistics/mental-health-statistics-suicide> [Accessed 1 May 2022].

13. CALM, 2022. *CALM—Campaign Against Living Miserably.* [online] Campaign Against Living Miserably. Available at: <https://www.thecalmzone.net/> [Accessed 1 May 2022].

14. Whogivesacrap.org, 2022. *Our Impact.* [online] Uk.whogivesacrap.org. Available at: <https://uk.whogivesacrap.org/pages/our-impact> [Accessed 1 May 2022].

15. Treatwell, 2022. *Lifesaving Wax.* [online] Available at: <https://www.treatwell.co.uk/inspiration/lifesavingwax/> [Accessed 1 May 2022].

16. Arnould, E. J., and Price, L. L., 1993. "River Magic: Extraordinary Experience and the Extended Service Encounter." *Journal of Consumer Research* 20(1), 24–45.

17. Airbnb, 2022. *Support for Refugees Fleeing Ukraine.* [online] Available at: <https://news.airbnb.com/help-ukraine/> [Accessed 1 May 2022].

INDEX